From Pitchfork
to Pulpit

From Pitchfork
to Pulpit

Donna Brunko

Pleasant Word

Packaged by Pleasant Word, PO Box 428, Enumclaw, WA 98022. The views expressed or implied in this work do not necessarily reflect those of Pleasant Word. The author(s) is ultimately responsible for the design, content and editorial accuracy of this work.

ISBN 1-4141-0250-X
Library of Congress Catalog Card Number: 2004095601

Table of Contents

Prolouge

*P*rior to becoming Wisconsin residents, my husband and I often visited friends living in Sister Bay. Knowing Mildred and Aymond Anderson lived nearby we were delighted to receive an invitation to their home.

One evening we sat around the Anderson table playing a game of Crazy Eight. The evening ended as we devoured Mildred's scrumptious Strawberry pie and talked about past events in our lives and ministry. As Aymond recounted stories from his childhood, including particularly tender remembrances of his dad, our attention centered only on him.

Each time we spent together, I sat captivated as I listened to this master storyteller. His sharp mind and unique sense of humor increasingly intrigued me. I longed for the day when his life story could be in writing, so that others could reap the benefits I now enjoyed.

Our contact increased with Aymond and Mildred when we became residents of Sister Bay. Eventually, I asked Mildred if anyone had written Aymond's life story. She responded by saying, "No, but I wish they would." Having a keen interest in the history of those who have experienced more years than I have known, I decided if no one else is writing his story, I'll give it a try.

I yearned to learn from Aymond and eventually share his story with others. I wanted to know more about his early years and the basis for his integrity. What were his formative years like? Why did he choose ministry over farming? I wanted to hear additional stories from his sixty plus years of ministry. I especially hoped to discover his insights into ministry in the early 1930's in contrast to the end of the century.

Armed with a modest amount of courage, I approached Aymond and asked if I could interview him for a short article. He answered sincerely, but mistakenly, "Why me? I'm a nobody." I immediately informed him he is 'a somebody' and *not at all* boring.

Perhaps Mildred's encouragement caused him to go along with my plan. Neither of us knew at the time that my questions and his answers would eventually emerge into more pages than originally thought possible.

The sessions began, resuming each summer when we both returned to our homes following winters away from Door County. In the beginning, I assumed my efforts would cumulate in a brief article. Before long I knew that would be impossible, so we surged on. Aymond enjoyed talking about his background and relating his many stories, but occasionally he looked at me and exclaimed, "God must have something better for you to do than this."

While listening to him talk, I observed this dear man with his six-foot plus frame, topped with a crown of exceptional thick, white hair, I knew within I had been handed a God given privilege. His animated expressions, the twinkle in his eyes and instruction to me, "Now listen, I'm going to tell you something," caused time to lose meaning. Yet, in the midst of listening, recording, jotting notes and laughing, I realized I had not anticipated the blessing God had laid before me. Aymond reinforced within me the power of prayer and the necessity of never giving up in prayer. He revealed the meaning of compassion while exemplifying the power of love. In his humble way he showed me God can use even one who considers himself a 'nobody.'

Chapter 1

The Molding of a Pastor

The Cook County Jail in Chicago held a young black boy in its restraining grip. Convicted of murder, he feared his upcoming sentence could result in the termination of his life strapped to the electric chair.

Joseph Frances, along with other prisoners, gathered daily in the 'Bull Pen' located near their cells. It was here that Moody Bible students held worship services for the many prisoners. Joseph listened intently when a student told about God's love for every one, no matter what their sin. When he heard the good news about this incredible love, he readily confessed his sin, received God's forgiveness, and gratefully received Christ as his very own Savior. Aymond Anderson, a Moody student in the late 1920's, regularly visited Joseph in the jail setting. In this confining and dismal place he explained the scriptures to Joseph, helping him understand his newfound faith.

The other inmates soon learned to respect Joseph. One morning as Aymond came to visit the prisoners, one of them anxiously approached Aymond asking if he had heard the news. The prisoner explained, "A meeting is scheduled in Springfield for Joseph with the board of pardon and parole. We've taken up a collection for you to go to Springfield and appear on his behalf." He then handed Aymond a donation of nickels and dimes. Aymond rationalized inwardly, "Who am I to appear before such a body as this board? I'm just off the farm." Then he resolved, "God will have to help me."

Trusting God for confidence and courage, Aymond traveled to Springfield. On the day of the hearing for Joseph and two others facing executions, Aymond entered the boardroom and sat with families and friends of the victims. The family of one of the other young men had hired a fine lawyer who presented his case.

Unfortunately his defense appeared hopeless. At the conclusion, the chairman of the board asked if any others would like to speak on the prisoner's behalf.

A woman stood and walked before the board. She knelt before them weeping with a mother's broken heart; she pled for her son's life. Others also began to cry. The mother's pleading went without effect, as her son's case indeed proved without hope.

Next, it was Aymond's turn to speak for Joseph. He described the transformation that had taken place in Joseph's life when he became a Christian and gave his life to Christ. He emphasized the effect of his new life on the other prisoners, and the respect and love they held for him. Sadly, Aymond's words proved futile.

That day in the courtroom Aymond marveled at the sobbing and distress he witnessed. In the midst of all the sadness surrounding him, he silently questioned, "Why are these people so distraught over some one the court decided is not fit to live? What is it about him, that gave him such value?"

Soon Joseph's life ended in the dreaded chair, but the courtroom experience made a lasting impression on Aymond. He continued to ponder about the value of this young man's life. Unknowingly, that day in the boardroom God firmly planted a seed of compassion in Aymond's young life. The seed sprouted and became part of Aymond's very nature; eventually flowing from the pulpit, guiding his hospital visitation and motivating his actions on city streets. Through this experience the foundation of Aymond's first sermon became "The Value of a Human Being."

The question must be asked, "what was the value system that shaped this 'green as grass,' shy, young farmer into one whom had the courage to even consider preparing for the ministry. One, who eventually became a captivating, sought after speaker?

The answer will be found when we learn how God led his footsteps.

Chapter 2

Home Sweet Home

$\mathcal{A}$ymond, who describes himself as a 'nobody,' entered this life Oct. 17, 1906. Born in the home of his parents, Willie, and Anna Anderson, he followed three other children, Raymond (who died at 10 months), Margie and Inez. Myrtle and Alice ultimately completed the family unit. At this time they lived in the modest farming community of Grandy, MN located about 65 miles north of Minneapolis, Minnesota. When Aymond was 4 1/2 years old the family moved to Parkers Prairie, MN, traveling by train; all their possessions packed in one large trunk.

Although Aymond scarcely recalls the Grandy home, a vivid memory lingers from these early years creating nightmares for him, which continued into adulthood. Occasionally, the farmers failed to secure their fences properly. Naturally, the bulls took advantage of their unexpected freedom and regularly escaped.

Unaware of a runaway nearby, Aymond and his sister hurried outside to play following lunch. Running around a large woodpile they encountered a gigantic white bull, an escapee from a neighboring farm. While the bull glared at them, two terrified children, with hearts pounding ran for their Dad who lost no time coming with a pitchfork chasing the animal away.

The promise of better farming lured Aymond's dad to move his family 175 miles northwest of Minneapolis and settle on 120 acres of farmland in Parkers Prairie, MN. This town must have seemed a burdensome distance from Grandy, especially to Aymond's mother.

His remarkable mother packed the family's few belongings. Along with her little children she accompanied her husband to an unseen, unknown area, unaware of the future awaiting them. Armed with a strong faith in God, she trusted Him to provide all of their needs. Aymond, too young to know about the purchase agreement, felt his Dad must have assumed buildings stood on the land. When the family of seven with their meager belongings, arrived at their new farm, they discovered to their astonishment that the 120 acres did not include a single building.

Apparently, not an unsolvable dilemma! At the invitation of a kindly neighbor, Oscar Lindquist, the Anderson family moved into the upstairs of his home until an all-purpose building could be built. How did Mrs. Anderson manage her 'little' brood while living in the home of another family and sharing the kitchen with another woman? Aymond proudly claims his mother always seemed 'on top of things,' had a good sense of humor and never showed stress! Could it be she raised a son much like herself?

Not one to waste time, Mr. Anderson, with the help of neighbors began construction on the building holding the highest priority. The cows, horses, and chickens needed shelter. Mr. Anderson's building plan included one room placed in the center of two attached sheds. The family would live in the center room and the animals, including the chickens were allotted the two sheds on either side.

A fine log house to keep the family cozy and warm might have been the Anderson's dream. Instead, when the walls eventually were erected they resembled hard cardboard. Thin wallboard nailed to the studs comprised the walls. Without insulation, the icy, cold, winter wind threatened to storm its way into their little home, the walls making only a feeble attempt to halt it's entrance.

Many years later Aymond returned to his roots in Parkers Prairie located one-mile north and two miles west of the town. The farm buildings, including the room he called home, had seriously deteriorated. A local doctors wife, interested in history, heard how the family of seven had lived in this one room, surviving the savage Minnesota winters. Desiring others to hear the story, she had the room moved into a sheep barn to preserve it. When Aymond visited the farm, he measured the room, where the family of seven lived. To his amazement the size was 16' x 24.'

Memories of waking to the sounds of crowing roosters blended with cackling hens and mooing cows, are imprinted on Aymond's mind. Many winter mornings the outside temperature plummeted to 40 below zero. The thin cardboard walls (minus the insulation of today) proved poor competition against the Minnesota winters, offering little warmth and comfort for the family.

A large, black, wood range provided their one source of heat and took up a sizable section of space. When Mrs. Anderson didn't have bread baking in the oven, the children propped their feet on the oven door hoping to warm them. All the meals were cooked on top of the wood stove. Water stayed hot while occupying the reservoir located on the side of the stove. Alas, as the fire diminished during the night hours, the pail of drinking water donned a covering of ice.

When the wind blew from a certain direction, the smoke reverted back into the room. The chimney had not been properly built and the resulting smoke created another ordeal for the family, Each pair of eyes stung unbearably, but with no other means of escape, they could only endure it.

On bitter cold mornings when the icicles hung outside the window with no hope of thawing, and the big wood stove took its time warming the families single room, Aymond's mother kept the children in 'bed' until ten o'clock. By then the stove had kicked in and sufficiently warmed their little home. The sleeping arrangements left ample room for improvement, but the family 'rose to the occasion.' His parents claimed the one bed in their home, and the children each slept on two chairs placed together. Blankets placed on the chairs aided in a degree of 'comfort' while horse blankets, plus a few 'regular' ones kept the children snugly warm. Easily satisfied, Aymond claimed "it felt so good!"

The frigid winters provided proof of the family's durability. Other challenges gave additional evidence when accidents and health problems occurred. They didn't have to travel to an 'unheard' of emergency room, as it was located in their efficient and creative living quarters. Without a telephone, they relied on their own wisdom.

Aymond recalls his father stepping on a board with a long, protruding nail during the construction of the building. His dad cried out in pain as the nail pierced his shoe, traveling into his foot and making its way through the top of his shoe. Call the town doctor? Not this durable and resourceful man! He took a strand of his wife's yarn and soaked it in liniment. Next he threaded a long needle, and sewed back and forth until the damage was repaired! "It healed well!" according to his son.

In another incident Mr. Anderson decided to pull out a tree stump. He tied two horses to a long pole, attached to a drum. This created immense tension and the pole snapped and broke, hitting him in the legs. He suffered severe bone injury as a result. Years later, Aymond speculated about the accident saying, "I can't help but wonder if the injury could have caused the Tuberculosis bacteria to enter my Dad's bones and eventually travel to his lungs."

The populace of Minnesota appeared as tough as the winters they survived. Aymond tells of a local man whose horse had thrown him, causing serious injury to his leg. In the Alexandria hospital the doctors felt it necessary to amputate his badly wounded leg! The family physician, Dr. Liebold, felt more capable of producing a satisfactory outcome without amputation. Even though he had difficulty with stuttering, he confidently told the 'big doctors' at the hospital, "le-e-t-t m-me t-try." So try he did and painstakingly stitched all the tendons and shattered pieces together himself! The result revealed expertise as it healed without infection.

Aymond's mother similarly demonstrated her sufficient pioneering toughness. Finances didn't allow for hospital treatment when she required a tonsillectomy. Consequently, 'there is no place like home' for such a procedure! Her 16x24 kitchen/emergency room became the surgical arena where the town doctor took care of the ailing tonsils.

The same held true when Aymond's sister busily ground leaves in an old meat grinder. The grinder lay in a box of junk Mr. Anderson had bought at an auction. Reaching her hand in too far, her fingers collided with very sharp blades, slitting four of her fingers and nails. As usual, the resourceful Mrs. Anderson took the 'cure all' liniment from the kitchen shelf applied it to her daughter's wounded fingers and bound them with clean strips of cloth. Aymond says, "I can still see my sister lying in bed, holding her hand in the air to ease the throbbing." Without a doubt, the fingers healed minus complications.

In the mid 1900's, Tuberculosis began to rage in all its fury throughout the community and nation. A neighbor from Parkers Prairie and two of his sons, both classmates of Aymond's died as a result of contracting the disease. After living in Parkers Prairie only one year, Aymond's dad sadly became very ill with the disease.

As a young child, Aymond didn't fully comprehend the manifestations of this dreadful disease. But, when his dad's condition deteriorated, making it necessary for him to enter the TB sanitarium, the picture is clearly etched on his mind. The 'San' was located 40 miles from their home. "When he left for the sanitarium, we children cried and cried," Aymond said, reflecting on this extremely traumatic day. He continued, "That same afternoon men came and fumigated the house. This process took overnight to complete, so we all slept in the haymow as a barn had recently been built by neighbors."

Due to the distance, forty miles from home, the children visited their dad only once. Aymond remembers the white room; white walls, stark white bed sheets and blankets; white bed-

spreads and towels. The patients wore white stocking caps for
warmth, as the windows were kept open for fresh air treatment.
On the bedside table sat little square cups, with lids that flipped
open, ready to hold the patients coughed up sputum. This dis-
tasteful and colorless picture only added to the family's dismay.
The most difficult part of the entire unsettling picture was of
their beloved dad lying ill on a bed that was not his own.

The family could not be at his bedside when death claimed
Mr. Anderson. His body was brought home in a pauper's coffin
shaped like a human. On arrival, it was placed in the tool shed.
A service held at the Baptist church had few in attendance. "Following our mother's example, we did not cry as no one wanted
to make it more difficult for the others." His beloved dad's body
was buried on Aymond's 8th birthday.

A prized possession of Aymond's is a letter to the children
from their ill father.

"My children

Margie, Inez, Aymond, Myrtle, Alice,

I'll write a few lines and tell you Papa thinks of you every day and I think it is too bad that I can't write more. I
hope you know papa is not so strong. You know when
papa was home, he did not write anything, but I will try
to do the best I can. I hope you have fun—help mama
all you can. I pray to God every day and night so you
must not think papa has forgotten you.
No, God is ours and we can ask anything we wish and
like.
Good-bye, my darlings,

Papa."

Aymond's mother took on the unwelcome identity of a widow
with five children to raise and support; a heavily mortgaged farm
and an unknown future. Even though a widow's pension was

available, she refused it saying, "With God's help I will make it on my own." Armed with a good financial head, she sold all the horses except one, and rented the farm 'on shares' to neighbors. This meant she would receive 1/3rd of the shares and the renter 2/3rd's.

Make it, she did! The family had little of this world's extras. Yet, at great personal sacrifice she made certain each of her children had the equivalent of a college education. This remarkable woman, named "Mother Of the Year," by the Parkers Prairie village, had taught school in Sweden. She lost the right to teach in that country when she gained her right to new life in Jesus Christ.

Many years later the section of town where Aymond's mother grew up celebrated their 100th anniversary. A cousin of Aymond's traveled to Sweden for the occasion. Upon his return, he showed Aymond an anniversary book he brought home. In the book is a special picture of Mrs. Anderson teaching her class of children.

All four of the Anderson girls taught school at one time. Eventually, one became a nurse and another a technician at PS Dupont. The other two continued as career teachers, and Aymond became a pastor. Aymond along with his sisters earnestly quote Abraham Lincoln, "All that we are or ever hope to be, we owe to our angel mother."

Relying on her God given inner strength, Mrs. Anderson found it necessary to undertake certain undesirable responsibilities. One day she heard noises in the attic above their one room home. Scampering claws overhead produced a noise most women prefer not to hear, let alone conquer. She felt the perpetrator should be seized immediately and she bravely climbed the steps to the attic. At the top of the steps, a rat suddenly jumped out of a toolbox and Mrs. Anderson reached to grab it with her bare hands. Mercifully, the rat was the faster one. Aymond said, "Thankfully, she didn't catch it or the rat could have bit her, injuring her badly."

The children's 'papa' had encouraged them to 'have fun.' They loved playing in the yard of 'the old homestead.' Not owning a single toy, they created their own fun. An enormous horseshoe of lilac bushes surrounded a large, round, earthen floored 'room' where the girls played 'house.' Lilac trunks shaped the walls and green foliage constituted the roof of their unique and private play area. When the spring season brought new life to the farm and left the cold winter season a memory, the playroom became filled with the fragrance of purple lilacs.

Aymond tried to suppress a grin when describing some of his youthful mischief, but the twinkle in his eyes overruled. His impish behavior had its birth during the preschool years. Growing up on a farm offered many opportunities to mix fun with a little creativity.

Armed with eggs and a bit of mischief, Aymond and his sisters headed to the watering area where the cattle and horses quenched their thirst. A hand pump forced water into a trough, where it flowed into a large tank. Two of the sisters raised the heavy handle up and down causing the water to pour forth. The other two gleefully broke egg after egg, watching the yolks flow down the 'river.' Mercifully he couldn't recall his parents reaction!

The children relished playing 'scary' games. Aymond alarmed his sisters when he teasingly told them he had just seen a tiger, when in reality it was the old tomcat. More innocent fun led the children to the large pasture where they played Hide and Seek, Pump, Pump Pull Away and Kick the Can.

Tall oak and poplar trees grew in the pasture where nearby gooseberry and hazel bushes grew. This provided tasty jam, cookies, and income for the family. Nearby a row of twelve large, gnarled, crab apple trees stood, marking the remains of an orchard whose trees continued to bear fruit. Along with picking gooseberries from prickly shrubs (a duty Aymond detested), the children had the responsibility of gathering luscious red apples in the fall. Their mother canned many jars of jam and jelly besides trading the produce for groceries at the local store; saving any scarce money she may have obtained.

After long and challenging winters, the hope of spring permeated the air. The winter snows began to thaw, flowing into the hollows creating ice thick enough to be rigid, yet appearing to bow with the movement of water on its surface. A feeling of excitement filled the children as they hiked to the hollows, put on their skates and tried out the 'rubber ice.' The warming breezes assured them welcome spring was on the way. Aymond's memories aren't too fond of this time though, as "the worn leather straps that supposedly held the skates on my feet, never stayed in place."

Skating in the fresh, crisp air only encouraged insatiable appetites. The children knew their mothers' wood cook stove would warm their chilled bodies, and the tantalizing aroma of freshly baked bread and cookies would fill their hungry stomachs. Aymond, recalling the wonderful fragrance, claims they always had "lots of fresh bread to eat, spread with homemade jam." Mrs. Anderson's kitchen evidently converted from an emergency room to a bakery then back to a bedroom as the circumstance demanded.

Games, skating and farm responsibilities filled the weekdays for Aymond and his sisters. On Sundays, the family seldom attended church, as they didn't own a car. Occasionally, a neighbor drove to the Anderson's in his Model T car and took the family to services at the Lutheran church. Mrs. Anderson made certain the children received spiritual teaching in their home. Each night a memorable time occurred when she tucked each child into their chair beds, and read the Bible to them by the dim light of a kerosene lamp. Following the scripture reading they listened while their mother prayed; usually in Swedish, which the children understood. The spiritual foundation of young Aymond Anderson became firmly rooted through his committed mother.

Another strong imprint on Aymond, occurred when neighbors and their children met together in each other's homes to pray. They didn't have a pastor or a leader, but simply met for prayer and to share personal experiences they had with Jesus. During these meetings, the spiritual groundwork established in Aymond's home became strengthened. As the children listened, they observed in the adult's a sincerity in their faith. As an active, young boy, Aymond denies boredom at these home meetings, saying "I loved to hear the older folks pray."

The importance of giving not only of our time, but the best we possess, became an indelible imprint on Aymond's life. One Christmas Eve, singing was heard outside his home. When he opened the door, he saw a group of church people singing Christmas carols and bearing gifts for the family. They had come by sleigh bringing 'boxes of good things.' "I remember how glad I was to get them," Aymond said thoughtfully, "but when we opened them all the toys were broken." Later in life he reflected how sad to give to another (or to the church) what is useless to us. He thought of II Samuel 24:24 that says, ". . . I will not sacrifice to the Lord my God, burnt offerings that cost me nothing." (NIV)

Despite gifts of broken toys, Aymond and his sisters enjoyed hanging up their stockings imprinted with their names. They hung on nails projecting from the wall and were the solitary decoration in the home. His mother did her best to give the children a special Christmas, baking cookies, and knitting stockings and mittens for the children. So they knew their stocking would be filled with gifts of love. An orange was an expected treasure to look forward to. A special gift that pleased Aymond one Christmas was, believe it or not, a little mousetrap!

"I really didn't know we were poor and at no time did I feel deprived," he said with meaning. "One day I saw a boy with an ice cream 'comb' and didn't know what it was. By and large, we were happy as a family." Year's later Aymond finally enjoyed a Christmas tree. "I guess so!" he laughingly related, "but not until I married Mildred."

He recalled one time, though, when hunger pains caused the children to search for food. Opening the cupboards only proved they were barren. Mrs. Anderson had taken the horse and buggy into town to exchange eggs and gooseberries for flour and sugar. She arrived home later than expected and realizing her children's concern for her, as well as their hunger, immediately set about baking bread and rice pudding. Aymond sighed, remembering the relief and happiness they felt knowing their mother was safe home with them and happily, about to feed them!

The grocery store where she occasionally shopped and traded was a 'one stop shopping center.' Possibly 100 items could be purchased from articles in the barrels sitting on the floor, or from the many shelves behind the counter containing canned goods. Flour, sugar, and coffee were sold in large sacks. Clothing, shoes, and yard goods awaited the customers in the back of the store. A black pot-bellied stove warmed the room and offered a cozy area for the locals to catch up on the latest town news. Even a few hardware items could be purchased.

The big night of the week occurred Saturday evening when 'everyone' came to town. In the midst of the bustling people shopping and greeting one another, the town barber kept busy giving the farmers their weekly haircuts.

Spiritual training from a godly mother, playing, and teasing his sisters, as well as ongoing mishaps amassed to make home on the farm a cherished, albeit humble existence to ponder with tenderness. Soon, his life would take on another dimension.

Chapter 3

Readin,' Writin' and Mischief

At seven years of age, Aymond the farm boy walked a short distance to a one-room school located in district #50, adjacent to the Anderson farm. Here he began his education along with an assortment of elementary students of various ages and grades. The children became enveloped in a commendable method of teaching and learning providing many memories and an excellent education. Sometimes, Aymond was the only pupil in his grade.

Although the building was small, it was modern enough to have a furnace in the basement. Keeping in tune with the 'times,' the use of bathroom facilities meant a path to an outdoor 'john.' When asked about his recollection of this open-air experience, he stated emphatically, "Cold, just like here, where I have the best john in Door County!"

Thirty to forty students received their instruction from one teacher. Among the teachers who taught Aymond were Edith Quam, Ida Moll and Agnes Hole.

Aymond remembered all the teachers were well dressed, but quickly recalled the life-long impact they left with him. Ida Moll was one of the teachers who began each day with prayer, followed by leading the children in "grrrreat songs, super, super!"

he said quite emphatically. "We sang hymns and songs contain-ing strong moral values." To illustrate, he began singing one of his school songs on the evils of alcohol,

"Touch not the Cup,
Touch not the cup, it is death to the soul,
Touch not, touch not.
Many I know who have quaffed from that bowl,
Touch not, touch not.
Little they thought that the demon was there,
Blindly they drank and were caught in the snare,
Then of that death-dealing bowl, oh beware,
Touch not, touch not."

Aymond's future ministry revealed the impact of this par-ticular song, as the subject frequently materialized in his ser-mons

The atmosphere in the one room, all 'grades together' school, proved an education in itself. Every student could hear each lesson taught from first to eighth grade as well as the other kids reciting. When Aymond's turn came to stand up and read ("reaaaad, you know"), the teacher, often busy, didn't completely 'tune' in as the children read. He grinned mischievously, "I often skipped big portions of the lesson knowing she couldn't follow everything." He thought this a fun thing to pull off, but admits that because he was a good student the teacher probably chose to ignore his antics.

Most of the children carried lunch pails to school, but Aymond lived close by, so he walked home for lunch. Enviously, he watched the other children remembering that their lunch pails were full of sandwiches and goodies. "They could always eat something, even at recess," he recalled in a voice that in-cluded a note of yearning from the past.

Each child had responsibilities to fulfill during the school day. Aymond took his turn drawing drinking water at the wood-shed pump. At the end of the school day he took the erasers outside, whacking them together as the chalk powder burst into a cloud of white dust.

During Aymond's second year of school, America's focus turned toward the war in Germany as World War I exploded. Patriotism filled the nation's heart with an intense passion. The American flag flew proudly, representing hard fought freedom. Numerous means of raising money for war bonds took place. Auctions became one method of collecting the needed funds. Personal items were most popular when auctioned for the 'cause' A skilled auctioneer, B. G., who 'really put life into his show' sold a rooster for $25.00, "a high price at the time, but the war effort was at stake," Aymond recalled. "In today's market it would equal $100.00."

Box socials also proved an exciting event, the proceeds going to aid the war effort. Women filled shoeboxes with homemade goodies and creatively decorated them. Secrecy reigned, as the ladies didn't want anyone to know who prepared it.

One particular box social held at the school struck Aymond's 'funny bone.' The teacher probably tipped off her 'special interest' young man about the description of her carefully decorated box. As the bidding started, the informed young man began at a hopeful $.25. Next, a neighbor bid against him raising the price another quarter. Finally, as they continued outbidding each other, the bid reached $12.00. At that point, someone in defense of the young man, shouted, "Let him have it!" The young man got the box, but alas, the romance failed to develop.

The war years brought more than fund raising socials to the little community where Aymond lived. These years demanded young men take an active part in the war, raging in unfamiliar lands. Not knowing if they would see their loved ones again, they bid them goodbye at the train station with loving hugs and lumps in their throats. Aymond doesn't recall seeing anyone crying. Instead, a rah, rah atmosphere prevailed as others cheered the 'boys' on. Shouts of "Whip the German's!" reverberated throughout the station. A popular ditty became:

"Kaiser Bill went up the hill,
To get a look at France.
Kaiser Bill came down the hill,
With bullets in his pants."

The school did their part to instill a patriotic spirit in the
children's mind and heart. A program held in the school building created an unexpected commotion. A campfire concocted
for the purpose of a visual aid was intended to burn for a half-
hour. A can of 'stuff' similar to gunpowder was placed in a pan
and ignited with a match. Rather than the intended glowing fire,
it gave a sudden pouf, and ended the planned object lesson in a
matter of seconds. Serious injuries by an explosion could have
occurred, but the unintentional sputter created a memorable
picture for young Aymond.

Aymond sadly recalled how in the midst of patriotic fervor,
innocent children of German descent felt the scorn and ridicule
from the American children. "This," according to Aymond's ob-
servation "caused them to undergo tremendous guilt and as a
result school fights regularly occurred."

Willie Mall and Willie Thun, became one example of the
frustration and distress these children felt. Willie Mall stood at
one end of the long school hall while Willie Thun, the larger of
the two, took the opposite end. He angrily threatened Willie
Mall, holding out his large hands, and shouted, "You put your
head right here." Big hands doubled into fists, as they angrily
shouted at one another, "I'm going to kill you!" Gratefully the
teacher appeared and no one was killed! "As I look back,"
Aymond mindfully added, "I realize the wrong we heaped on
these children, and now I feel sorry for them."

With the signing of the Armistice, the German children kept
a low profile as many of their relatives still lived in their home
country. This created an additional fear within their young hearts.
Needless to say, the rest of the children celebrated. The boys
jubilantly rang the school bell, breaking the rope in their youthful exuberance. Not wanting the ringing interrupted, Aymond

along with another boy came to the rescue and climbed up the roof to the belfry continuing the joyful ringing by hand.

Readin' and Writin' must continue in spite of the celebration bursting forth. Included in the life of any school, discipline occasionally became necessary. During Aymond's elementary years, the culprit had to stay after school or stand chagrined, in the corner. Aymond, the excellent student and future pastor, admits to experiencing the consequences of improper behavior. He concedes to 'lots of fist fights,' as a result of a self-proclaimed temper. "You bet, I had a temper; I'd kill the guys," he laughed. Today, he considers those past fights, 'no big deal,' even though one fight ended with a bloody nose for him and another the pain of a broken nose. Unquestionably he experienced the inevitable outcome at the hand of his teacher, and perhaps his loving mother.

Aymond chose not to tell about the teacher's discipline, but instead described how his mother applied discipline to the seat of learning. When the children misbehaved, she sent them outside to cut a switch. "I sure didn't return with a 2 x 4, but made certain to choose a fine willow twig; big mistake! Boy, did that sting," he painfully recalled.

Aymonds mischief didn't confine itself to home. "One day I played a trick on the teacher," he grinned. "You want to hear about it?" (Of course). He continued, "I found a turtle, wrapped it in a box and brought it to the teacher. She was holding a little kid on her lap. I explained the mailman had just left this box for her. She opened it, let out a scream and dropped the kid," he said, laughing heartily.

Not only do his antics paint a picture of the past, but also school events provide colorful memories. Even though the Anderson family didn't have the luxury of a Christmas tree, one adorned the schoolhouse. The children helped decorate the tree and loved to string popcorn into long garlands coiling them around the tree making the room festive for the Christmas season.

With much excitement the children practiced for the school's Christmas program. Families watched as the children enthusiastically presented skits, recited poems, and sang Christmas songs. Santa Claus made an eagerly anticipated appearance each year at the program. One year though, the children fearfully kept their distance. Santa Claus arrived not wearing the expected red suit, but instead had donned a sheep lined over-coat turned inside out, and a home made mask. In 'real life' the children loved this man.

A portion of the poem Aymond recited at the program came easily to his memory

"Santa came down the chimney,
Quick, quick, quick.
Left nothing but a stick.
Mother said 'twas because I acted naughty
???????"

Perhaps he preferred not to recall the entire poem or could it be there was a reason this poem was his to recite!

Antics set aside temporarily, Aymond decided to help his mother with her financial needs. As a result at age 10, he entered the 'work world.' Haying season began his 'career' and he became a farm hand. His first assignment was the unpalatable duty of cleaning the barn. He also milked the cows, minus compensation for his duties, simply the reward of helping his mother.

A few years later, a nearby farmer knowing his dependable work reputation, hired him for $.25 cents an hour plus room and board. "All summer I stood in awe of this very stern man," Aymond reminisced. His first paying employer had fought during the civil war and in a conflict with the Indians, all of which added to Aymond's respectful apprehension of him.

Aymond and the farmer's son slept in a tent near the farmhouse, which he recalls as a 'neat' experience. The tent flaps whipped and the walls seemed to hum when a strong wind blew. Occasionally, the summer rains came in torrents, pouring down on the roof onto the sides of the tent, threatening to soak both boys.

When the dinner bell rang, the hungry farm hands grimy from their farm work headed for the barrels of rainwater standing outside the farmhouse. They poured water from the barrels into the basins perched on stands. When dutifully scrubbed and ready for lunch, they entered the screened porch of the home and sat down to eat. The farmhouse itself remained quite a mystery, as Aymond never received an invitation to enter farther than the porch.

The austere farmer staunchly opposed smoking. When the boy's curiosity got the better of them, they figured behind the barn was the only place to experiment. One day the other hired hand, who rolled his cigarettes, went into town on an errand. The two young farm hands took advantage of his absence and tried rolling 'a couple.' Using whatever paper was available, they wrapped it around oak leaves. "You know when you're hungry for a smoke anything will do," Aymond joked. With a sense of realism he added, "I smoked just a few puffs, and got such a headache, I had to sit under a tree for awhile. That was the end of my smoking and I'm eternally grateful."

Aymond's elementary years ended in 1918 as did the troubled years of WWI. However a new crisis cast its somber shadow in the midst of the celebrations. The horrendous influenza epidemic began its prey on people throughout the world, causing the death of twenty-two million worldwide. Sadly, schoolmates of the Anderson children and a young grocer in Parkers Prairie were among those who didn't survive the flu. Servicemen abroad, who had survived the war, now perished from the flu. When people left their homes they attempted to protect themselves by wearing masks. Public meetings, including church services had to be canceled. Thankfully, the Anderson family was not affected. It appeared the world had emerged from one boiling cauldron only to plunge into another.

Yet, even this latest crisis inevitably ended and life finally took on a sense of welcome normality and Aymond's education continued, as did the necessity of farm work.

Most students following their elementary years couldn't continue their education, as they needed to find available work. Aymond's mother understood the value of an education, and made it crystal clear to her children they would go on to high school. As a result, Aymond spent the next four years at Parkers Prairie High School, and continued to work on a farm.

School buses had not entered the picture as yet. The only transportation for Aymond was to ride his bike into town to attend high school. In a brief time, the subzero temperatures brought a halt to his biking. The next best arrangement provided room and board closer to town. Here he lived with a farm family, helping with the farm work, which paid for his keep. On weekends he returned home to his mother's cooking and a never ending love.

For farm boys desiring to attend high school, harvest season took precedence over school attendance. Because of this, Aymond and a few older boys (some in their twenty's), started school later in the fall. Aymond spent his days picking potatoes, already dug by others, and placing them in containers. The crops had to be harvested when ready, and the outside work completed before the temperature plummeted, depositing its icy crystals over the fields. Some boys could attend school only in the winter, leaving in the spring when heavy farm work began.

At the conclusion of harvest season, Aymond plunged into his studies trying to catch up to the other students. In spite of his love for athletics, he couldn't muster enough time for the required practice. Farm chores continually awaited the appearance of a farmer. Aymond also needed to earn his room and board. Football would have been out of the question as Aymond was a lightweight for that sport. Later in college years, basketball proved a sport he dearly loved.

Although a good student, Aymond's temper occasionally remained a problem. One day Aymond sat in the school study hall, innocently reading. Suddenly, his head met with a piece of chalk. The only other person in the room was Clem, another student. With a surge of indignation Aymond jumped up from his desk and chased Clem around the hall twice. In the midst of the chase he came face to face with one very strict principal. Clem presented his side of the story placing the blame on Aymond. The principal then turned to Aymond saying, "I understand you're one of the chief actors." Aymond replied, "I guess so." Despite an attempt at honesty and refusal to place the initial blame on Clem, Aymond's display of anger caused him a two-day suspension from school.

Aside from an admitted temper, Aymond seemed to possess a natural ability for the stage, making people laugh. As a result, he frequently appeared in school programs. His comedic abilities shone in humorous monologues portraying a black man. Making himself more realistic for the role, he applied burned cork to color his skin.

Despite his shortened school year due to farm work, his mischief, and living away from home during the winter months, Aymond graduated salutatorian of his high school class of 17 students.

Following high school he continued working several years as a farm hand. Aymond's farm years (some prior to graduation from high school) yielded some unique happenings.

His farmer employer asked Aymond (at the young age of thirteen), to care for the horses during haying time. This required him to stay on location 12 miles from the farm. All alone at night, without nearby neighbors, he attempted to sleep on a hay wagon tied to the horses. Lying under the stars and viewing God's incredible creation became vastly more important than sleep. Eventually the discomforts of his earthly existence proved a restless challenge. "During the first night" he recalled, "the mosquitoes nearly devoured me. I remedied that the next evening by throwing a horse blanket over a pitchfork and crawling under it. The mosquitoes left me alone and instead attacked the poor horses who then stomped their feet all night to shake them off."

One day the farmer left for a meeting 25 miles away. His son and Aymond remained behind operating the farm for several days. During the farmer's absence one of the horses became ill with lockjaw and didn't survive. The two young farmers knew they must bury the animal immediately due to the infectious disease.

It was winter and the solidly frozen ground proved a colossal challenge. As they considered their repulsive job, they decided their only option was to blast the ground for a burial spot. They purchased several sticks of dynamite, and using a crow bar to loosen the frozen ground, placed the dynamite to a depth of about 2 feet, tamping it into place with the crow bar. They then blasted away. Using a team of horses, they pulled the dead horse out of the barn. As they did this, a padding of manure and mud fell off the horse's hoof, revealing a piece of wire which had entered the animal's foot, infecting it and causing the disease. An even worse situation might have occurred though the boys did not recognize it then.

Thinking back on the method they used, Aymond voiced the dilemma that could have occurred as they tamped the dynamite in place with the crow bar. It could possibly have struck a stone, igniting a spark, resulting in a premature explosion. Both young men could have suffered serious injuries. At any rate, the two young farmers came through the crisis safely, and the horse had a proper burial complete with a future minister in attendance.

Another farm incident proved less fortunate for Aymond. When operating a carrier on a track used in cleaning the barn, a part of the carrier malfunctioned striking Aymond in the face and cutting his cheek so badly that a flap of skin hung below his right eye. This caused him to fall on the concrete floor knocking him unconscious. When he regained consciousness, he walked the distance to the farm home. The doctor came and stitched the laceration in the home emergency room known as the kitchen, naturally minus modern medical devices. He survived with his sight intact, but continues to bear a hardened area below his right eye.

Friends encouraged Aymond to begin farming on his parent's farm. This meant purchasing cows and pigs, horses and machinery. Farming had become a way of life for him, so he took their advice and managed to acquire a loan from the bank. All the years of working as a farm hand eventually paid off as he developed a prize herd of cows, a story deemed important enough for the local paper to report.

Soon the scene changed as the great economic depression began to crush many dreams. In addition, a period of drought came upon the land and anticipated rainfall never materialized, drying up the lakes. As a result, some of the farmers plowed the dry lakebeds for their crops, due to the richness of the soil. (Returning home many years later, Aymond witnessed that all the lakes had been restored and new ones had formed.)

Many farmers had no choice, but to give up farming during this dire time. Aymond described the depression era as 'awful.' Yet, everyone experienced the same dreadful situation and together they coped as best they could with the hope of surviving. Poor crops prevailed and prices plunged to almost nothing. Aymond also raised pigs and oats, receiving 1 1/2 cents a pound for the pigs, and 15 cents a bushel for the oats. "Just think of that 1 cent!" he recalled amazed.

Unknown to Aymond the farmer, God would soon reveal His "plans . . . to give him hope and a future," Jeremiah 29: 11

Chapter 4

A Divine Nudge

$\mathcal{M}$ilking cows, cleaning barns, planting and harvesting, seemed the natural direction of Aymond's life. During the impressionable school years, along with various church opportunities, his leadership, scholastic achievement and even stage competence confirmed the God given abilities that prepared him for the new direction his life would soon take.

Never to be forgotten influences left their mark on young Aymond. One day a godly neighbor, with a snow-white beard, quite distinct from his red, teary eyes, visited the Anderson home. He had become concerned for Mr. Anderson, Aymond's father, who had 'drifted away' from his spiritual convictions. Due to the loving and caring attitude he displayed, Aymond's dad rededicated his life to the Lord.

Did the neighbor with the red eyes ever realize the impact of his visit on the heart of this young boy? Perhaps not, but the compassion he showed when he took time to visit and share his faith, is remembered by Aymond decades later.

The spiritual teaching and example Aymond's mother exhibited in the home, most likely made the deepest imprint on him, "But at the time," he admits, "I didn't appreciate it as I do now." His mother frequently attended home prayer meetings taking her children along. Here other Christians left an indelible stamp on Aymond, part of God's plan to mold this young boy for a life of ministry.

The family seldom attended church services as they lacked transportation. This situation changed when Aymond's sister began teaching school and earned enough to purchase a car. Now they could drive to their modest, country church, large enough to seat about 100 people. To maintain the congregation's comfort during the frigid Minnesota winters, a few of the men kept a wood-burning furnace fired and ready to keep the congregation warm. Through the youth programs, Sunday school and the worship services of the church, God's hand continued to cast and shape the mold of a future preacher.

The little church held a week of evangelistic meetings coinciding with the time the Anderson family began attending. Aymond listened closely as a woman evangelist spoke clearly of her conversion from another faith sharing the positive changes that had taken place in her life. As a result of her new faith, her family treated her with rudeness, feeling convicted by the transformation they witnessed.

As Aymond gave ear to her testimony, he was deeply affected. Inwardly, he knew he was a child of God, mainly because of his mother's influence. He hadn't outwardly prayed to receive Christ as his Savior, yet knew he believed.

"I had a super-super mother, when you think of it," he said empathetically. "Left with five children and a heavily mortgaged farm to care for, she kept her head on her shoulders and set a firm goal that all her children would be educated!"

In spite of the evangelist's influence, he couldn't forget the inner questions that continued to nag him. "Satan would bug me with thoughts of 'how do you know you're a Christian?' as I couldn't refer to any time or place when I had made a decision. People also asked me the same question, so I decided to settle the matter and make it public."

The pastor of the Anderson's church conducted tent meetings one summer. Determined to follow through on his decision to make his faith public, Aymond 'walked the aisle' to the front of the tent. Even though he had an inner assurance that he knew Christ as his Savior, he longed for a time and a place he could refer to. He claimed, "This became an anchor in my faith. I knew I had done it. When 14 years old, he followed the Lord's command, and his pastor baptized him in Lake Hadley.

However, Aymond rarely attended church services.. When present, he listened with keen attention to the pastor's message. One sermon, "The Lowered Window Shade," pricked his heart creating a life-long impact. The main point of the message that Sunday, was allowing the Lord to be first in our finances. From that day on, tithing became a priority in Aymond's life and future ministry, as many of his messages he eventually prepared, spoke pointedly to this step of obedience.

His church attendance went from rare to regular when his pastor, Leo Sandgren, demonstrated a caring attitude towards him. Rather than chastising him for lack of church attendance, he demonstrated a loving attitude towards a teenager who didn't have a father. He visited Aymond at home and occasionally took him duck hunting, realizing the potential residing in his young parishioner. Pastor Sandgren became another person God used in shaping the mold of a young man destined to become a life long pastor.

"There were times, however, I stayed in my sister's Model T car reading the comics until the family left the services and we could drive home." Aymond continued, "I don't know why I did this as I really wasn't rebellious." The pastor, not discouraged, hung in. Rather, he encouraged Aymond to enter a contest for youth, based on the book of Acts and sponsored by the Minnesota Baptist Conference. Aymond agreed, entered, and won the contest in his local church. He then went on to the district and state contests, winning them both and creating a motivation within not previously noted. A sterling silver candlestick engraved with his name, date, and contest name is stored in an archive 'somewhere.'

Aymond's leadership qualities blossomed in his church under the strong influence of this caring pastor. All this, even though, "I was somewhat bashful. It was hard for me to walk in and face everyone."

He became the recipient of much unsolicited advice regarding his future. Some, aware of his leadership gifts, freely dispensed helpful, encouraging suggestions. On the other hand, others, such as his pastor's wife, offered less than helpful words when she advised him to become an undertaker. "You'd make a good one," she said. "Tall, dark and handsome, wearing a long black coat and pushing a casket down the aisle!"

Her husband gave a more providential opinion, saying simply to Aymond, "I think you'd make a good minister." These words made an impression on Aymond, and the thoughts remained steadfast through the work of the Holy Spirit.

Due to the economic depression of these trying years, it became difficult to continue farming. Aymond seriously began to question if the Lord could possibly be leading him in another direction? The pastor's recent words continued to crop up in his mind, causing uneasiness within. He found himself on the threshold of a life changing decision. Should he choose to make a living in the secular world, or yield to the Lord's call in ministry?

His wavering became a serious battle. He recalled the darkest, dreariest day of his life: "I was in the barn milking cows and felt as though engulfed in deep darkness. The burden became heavier until I got up, kicked the stool, and blurted out, 'Lord, I will do what you want me to do. I'm going with you.'" At that point he left the barn and strode into the house to let his very gratified mother know his decision.

Having toiled on a farm since 10 years of age, followed by managing his own farm, Aymond expected it would be his life long occupation. When his pastor learned of Aymond's recent decision to prepare for the Lord's work, he wisely advised him, stating pointedly, "You're 26 years old. You had better get going!" At the pastor's urging, Aymond intended to bypass college and enter Moody Bible Institute. He thought it best to begin his ministry before he was really old!

The emotional, but firm decision to 'go with the Lord' settled, Aymond needed to come off the mountaintop and consider the practicalities surrounding him. He had a farm to sell. True to His faithfulness, God provided the way. Soon, a man came to look over the farm, made a decision, and bought everything pertaining to the farm! Due to depression times, the sale offered a minimum amount of money, and little remained for the future student.

Aymond's mother had moved from the farm and now lived with her daughter Margie in Weyerhaeuser, Wisconsin. Business matters finally settled regarding the farm, farewells needed to take place. Some of them proved very difficult. When Aymond visited a man who had employed him in the past, the unexpected confronted him. This man had never displayed much zeal in his faith. He found it most difficult to say goodbye to Aymond and began to cry unashamedly. His rush of emotion 'crushed' Aymond, as he didn't have any idea the man cared for him. "It really broke me up and I too, began to cry."

After saying a final goodbye, he got in his car, leaving behind all he held dear from his youthful years. "I then drove 175 miles to my sister's home and cried the entire distance," he related.

Year's later Aymond held special meetings in the vicinity where his employer lived. In the congregation each night sat his friend who had driven close to one hundred miles to hear Aymond preach. At one of the meetings Aymond had the "awesome" experience of leading his friend to Christ.

Yes, 'God knew the plans He had' for Aymond's life.

Chapter 5

Getting Going

*E*xchanging the quiet, sheltered farming community of Parkers Prairie, MN, for the mega city of Chicago, caused Aymond to sense an insecure feeling of insignificance. As he stepped off the train he heard the loud noise of cars, buses and trucks whizzing by, their horns blaring impatiently. Yet, in spite of insecure feelings he couldn't help but marvel at how God had led him to attend Moody Bible Institute to prepare for the ministry. Years later, as he pondered this experience, he remarked, "I was green from the farm. It's a wonder I made it."

He soon learned life in Chicago meant exchanging fields of potatoes and a prize herd of milk cows, for concrete sidewalks and towering buildings. In contrast to the quiet, peaceful farmlands of Parkers Prairie, Aymond quickly became snared in the frenzied big city life and the whirlwind of school schedules. Surrounded by students in the dorm and classes, his quiet life had undergone a radical metamorphosis. As each day dawned, he and the other students 'gulped' a quick breakfast and rushed to their classes. At the conclusion, many made a hurried exit to their particular workplace, often prior to ministry assignments. At the end of a long, weary day, hours of study awaited the students.

Aymond, who at age fourteen had earned the title of the fastest potato picker, by picking 1400 bushels of potatoes one season; each worth a mere five cents a bushel, now bussed dishes in the Maryland Hotel. This fine restaurant located on the gold coast of Chicago hosted many conventioneers at their 60 tables. It was also a popular place for "the big guys," according to Aymond. The mayor, along with lawyers and those in the political arena, devoured many delectable meals while Aymond busily lugged trays of soiled dishes from the tables to the kitchen. This job, although mundane, provided Aymond the former farmer, with a room to sleep in and two meals a day.

Not privileged to own a car, Aymond's legs sufficed as his method of transportation. When his work hours ended, he walked to his dorm through 'Bug House Square,' a small park located near Moody. On one side of the area stood the Newberry Library. Mr. Newberry had donated the park area, stipulating that free speech and expression would be acceptable. As a result, great entertainment took place in the park as soapbox orators shouted their spiel, often pedaling the communist philosophy. Watching fire-eaters and jugglers perform their act, gave the passers-by on foot and in sightseeing buses, an enjoyable respite. These tired students probably needed this time to laugh and simply relax for awhile.

Dorm life at Moody initiated Aymond into an education he hadn't totally expected. A young man who thought it necessary to 'put down' everyone but himself, was assigned as Aymond's roommate. The opposite personality of Aymond, Norman created many problems for none other than himself.

One night as Aymond slept soundly in the upper bunk, he was startled awake by a loud noise created by a group of determined students. Minus any need for quiet they marched into Aymond and Norman's room and grabbed a startled Norman. They carried their struggling conquest to a prepared bathtub and gave him a ceremonial dunking. Eventually the 'guys' released poor Norman from his traumatic experience.

Humiliated, he walked back to his dorm room failing to see any humor in this degrading experience. Soaking wet and grasping a dripping wet slipper, his eyes overflowed with tears. Sobbing, he lamented his ill-fated plight to Aymond, vowing the 'Lord will take care of them.' Unsympathetically, Aymond failed to hide his laughter as he listened while observing poor Norman's condition. As he reminisced on this happening, he laughed again saying, "He got his due. Guys will take care of guys!"

Education at Moody transpired in locations other than the dorm and classroom. Ministering to people in one of Chicago's missions; interacting with the homeless and hopeless on the streets, and standing on street corners offering tracts to folks who passed by, all became a part of the students training. They experienced compassion as they visited with the inhabitants of the jails and hospital beds. Being a part of a ministry team in local churches, all contributed to the molding of future pastors and missionaries. "A grrreat experience," Aymond fondly recalls.

Aymond easily extracts stories of his student days from the archives of his incredible mind. On assignment at the Cook County Hospital, he visited patients, going from bed to bed, reading scripture, witnessing, and praying. During one of his bedside visits, he came to a man with a large face and extremely light blue eyes. After reading to him from the scriptures, Aymond began talking with him informally. The patient spoke to Aymond in a firm voice quoting John 4:26. He then said, "Don't talk to ME like that. Don't you know that I that speak to thee am He?" "He scared the wits out of me," Aymond said. "He actually thought he was Christ!" Startled, Aymond thought, "All is not well here! This guy is not for me, so I got out of there!"

While a student at Moody, Chicago's Mayor Cermak was assassinated. Aymond remembers this as a sad day for Chicago when their mayor was taken from them unexpectedly and tragically. A group of Moody students visited the cemetery where he was buried. There they found the entire area surrounding his grave covered with flowers, which had taken dozens of trucks to transport them to the graveside.

During this time, the city of Chicago became enveloped in a period of big gang activity. Al Capone, Ma Barker, Terrible Tommy Touhy, Pretty Boy Floyd, and John Dillinger were among the well-known gangsters. Later, in an abandoned building on N. Clark St., the Valentine day shooting and killing of nine gang members occurred.

Aymond's student ministry included an assignment to the Cook County jail. Here he preached to Tommy Touhy and his gang as they sat at tables in the bullpen. An invitation to receive Christ followed the sermon. If anyone raised a hand in response to the invitation, a follow up worker from Moody visited the inmate the next Sunday.

When John Dillinger was killed, his body lay in the Cook County morgue. Aymond thought it would be good to get additional information on the situation so he could tell the intriguing story to young people. When asked how he got access to the morgue and permission to view such a notorious person, his mischievous yet sheepish grin emerged and he replied, "Treacky, treacky."

Desiring a co-conspirator, he took another student with him. They came to the morgue where guards stood posted. The two students mustered up the necessary confidence and walked by them with an air of importance. When they approached another guard standing by the entrance, Aymond told him, "I'm going into the ministry and I'd like to tell this story to young people. It would be good to have something to attract their attention." Unbelievably, the guard allowed them entrance. Once they entered the morgue, they saw the dead body of the notorious Dillinger lying on a slab, his body, with the exception of his head, was covered with a sheet. Hence Aymond had another great story to illustrate a life gone wrong.

Living in the incomparable city of Chicago added many unforgettable experiences to 'Aymond's archives.' He attended the World's Fair several times during 1933 and '34; captivated by unbelievable scenes he could not have encountered in Parkers Prairie! Visiting the "Believe It Or Not Ripley Show," stands out in particular. A three-year-old girl had a protrusion jutting out of her side; part of another body with arms and legs, but not fully developed. Amazingly the little girl could run and play. Years later, attending the Minnesota State Fair, his curiosity drew him once again into the "Believe It Or Not" show. A nice-looking teenage girl stood on stage with the growth remaining on her side. The same girl!

Even as a student, Aymond was unceasingly aware of others, observing people with sympathetic compassion. He remembers stopping at a small restaurant for lunch on his way to work at the downtown Maryland Hotel. Seated at the counter, he turned and saw a man with his bare feet propped on the table. Shocked, Aymond knew this couldn't be proper etiquette, even on the farm. Just then the waitress approached the man and placed a plate of food before him. He then picked up his knife with one foot and proceeded to spread butter on his toast. At this point, Aymond, whose face reflected astonishment at the ability he witnessed, noticed the man didn't have arms. Many years after his experience in the restaurant, Aymond pastored the Lakeside Baptist Church in Wentworth, WI. The Tri-County fair was on in nearby Superior, WI. Aymond's fascination with the unbelievable brought him to the "Believe It Or Not" show once again. An unexpected feature included the same man he had observed in the restaurant. Demonstrating what he could accomplish with his feet, the man threw knives at a woman who stood against a wall (presumably, his wife. Such submission on her part, and apparently one never hit her!) Reliving the scene, Aymond says, "I couldn't believe I was seeing the same man. I will never forget this."

The years at Moody had a deep effect on this 'green from the farm' young man. During these years he claims, "I found myself. I realized I kind of had ability 'to do.' You know, you compare yourself with others. I took a course where we had to tell Bible stories and according to the teacher, I was the greatest! I needed to get my feet wet so as to gain confidence."

Yet, he longed to see his mother he held so dear. She lived with her daughter a distance from Chicago, so following a day of classes, Aymond traveled by train arriving late at night in an unknown town. No one met him at the station, so it was up to him to find his sister's home. He began walking, merely guessing at the direction to take. After a distance of seven miles in 'pitch' blackness he somehow found the right house. The late arrival, the unknown area and location became worth it all as he enjoyed two days visiting with his beloved mother. There were not to be too many more visits as his mother went to her heavenly home at age 71.

Aymond completed his education at Moody graduating in August of 1934. He felt equipped for ministry and he was eager to 'get going.' At that time, no opportunity for Christian service presented itself so he continued to bus dishes at the Maryland Hotel restaurant. Thankfully, God knew the plans he had for Aymond and another change began to unfold.

His high school teacher, Esther Sabel, now taught at Bethel College in St. Paul, Minnesota. Miss Sabel learned that Aymond had graduated from Moody and wrote to him suggesting he consider attending Bethel. As Aymond had contemplated whether he should further his education, her letter seemed to put a 'go for it' in his mind.

With $15.00 in his pocket and his future entrusted to God, Aymond began his first year at Bethel College. A meeting with Dean Walford Danielson was top on his priority list as it was imperative to discuss his financial situation. The Dean told him of a federal program providing aid to students in need; one that required the student to work. He offered him a job on campus and Aymond was set for another few years of education.

Grateful for employment, Aymond was placed in charge of student's seven years younger, but all shared a common financial need. Classes were the priority, and the work schedule had to fit in, but they managed to accomplish their tasks in many areas of the campus; maintaining the grounds and using their carpenter skills. Aymond's conscientious work and reliability didn't go unnoticed by the dean. As a result, he continued in this capacity for Bethel. After four years of school Aymond graduated without financial indebtedness; evidence of the Lord's faithful provision!

However, Aymond's classes and work never interfered with his education. Dorm life had a way of shaping character even then. His friend Clifford Dickau remembers Aymond as a crack shot with a water pistol, and a master at putting together bath-tub brews. This meant some unlucky student would be carried struggling into the tub room; then dunked in an unwelcome, cold concoction of ice water, ink, and occasionally other unholy ingredients.

A close knit group of six seminary students all from the same Greek class, armed themselves with water pistols. They used the Greek words Hooder Ballow (water throwers) as the distinctive of their group. The other seminary students didn't appreciate their arrogance, and they decided it best to deflate them. This resulted in the six arrogant students becoming good candidates for a dorm bathtub immersion.

Aymond remembers (as an instigator) one determined night, two teams of five each stormed the dorm to get the six egotistical students. Armed with Hooder Ballows, they barged into their rooms, tied them up, and painted the initials HB on their foreheads. The helpless students one by one were unceremoniously carried into the tub room. Further humiliation was heaped on them as they unmercifully landed in a bathtub filled with the usual icy mixture.

Another student hoping to avoid the inevitable bathtub experience locked himself in the bathroom. Those outside the door wasted no time as they helped another student climb through the transom window, and unlock the door for the team who immediately barged in and carried out their mischievous plan.

After all the bathtub parties Aymond instigated and/or participated in, the question to ask is when did his turn come? Aymond, with a grin that divulges the delight he still feels in these antics, tells of his fateful night. "They tried to get me, but I'd barricade myself in my room, making it impossible for anyone to burst in." Alas, graduation was nearing and unknown to Aymond, a plan was in the making. "Many of the students had a church meeting to attend, so I figured no one would come that night." Consequently he failed to put the barricade on the door before going to sleep. "Suddenly, a bunch of guys burst in, grabbed me and I got dunked!" He grinned and admitted he got his due!

Returning from a speaking engagement late one night Aymond wearily climbed the steps to his dorm room. One of the students loved to drink milk and when the bottles were empty he placed them neatly outside his door. Aymond spied the bottles ahead in the long hallway. To his delight a shot-put ball sitting at the top of the stairway offered significant temptation and suddenly his energy returned. Unable to resist, he rolled the ball toward the milk bottles and made a direct strike. The bottles all exploded and glass like shrapnel flew all over. The bowling culprit ran into his room and no one discovered who created the mischief!

Mischief seemed at the core of Aymond's being and he easily used it like a professional, usually without penalty. Grocery bags filled with luscious fruit 'safely' sat on the windowsill of a corner dorm room. The student thought this a safe place where they would keep cool. Unfortunately the master of mischief spied them. Yielding to temptation seemed the only option. Another student aided in the theft and they managed to open a hall window. Using their long arms, they stretched around the outside wall and managed to reach the windowsill where they easily snatched the bags of fruit. Of course, the elusive Aymond, while biting into a delicious apple, enjoyed picturing the student returning to his room, mouth watering in anticipation of enjoying a juicy piece of fruit.

In addition to classes, mischief, and working Aymond kept extremely busy as president of many organizations, i.e., student council, his class and male chorus. All of these activities added to a solid foundation for future leadership. His love for athletics drew him into baseball, handball, and Bethel's championship volleyball team.

Two years at Bethel College plus an additional two years at Bethel Seminary continued to prepare Aymond for many years ahead of pastoral ministry. As at Moody, he gained helpful experience speaking in public. Yet, a first preaching assignment can spark terror even into the best!

Aymond remembers his first experience when as a Bethel student he preached at the Fort Madison, Minnesota church.

Even though he had preached in missions, jails and on street corners, a church in contrast, seemed terrifying. He said, "I was so nervous while waiting in a side room. I peeked around the door and saw the congregation sitting and waiting. I almost did not go onto the platform. I wanted to turn and run." Regardless, preach he did, and preaching he does, as he faithfully continues into his 90 plus years!

Lakeside Baptist Church of Wentworth, Wisconsin became his first student pastorate. The church benefited from a pastor only when one became available from Bethel Seminary. Aymond served as pastor for four and one-half summer months at this church and describes it as a 'rich experience.' During other summers he preached when needed at Sandy Lake, MN, and Lake City, MN.

After a summer of pastoring, Aymond returned to Bethel. Not only did he fulfill his student obligations during the school year, but he also became part-time pastor of the Lake Park Baptist Church, located about a mile from campus. This small congregation benefited from his gift of preaching and ability to direct the choir.

During this pastorate, Aymond received a call from the Lakeside Baptist Church requesting him to conduct a funeral; Aymond's first. A young man, a 'pillar' of the church had drowned in a boating accident. Almost thirty years old, he had planned to be married in two weeks. Aymond knew the sudden death of one so young leaves friends and loved ones in a state of shock. What a responsibility to speak and bring comfort to those whose hearts were shattered so abruptly! But this inexperienced, student preacher, once again very nervous, brought comfort to the ones who desperately needed it, trusting the Lord to give him the words.

This student/pastor had 'got going' as his pastor had recommended. Aymond gave his best as he studied at Moody and continued further preparation at Bethel College and Seminary. God gave Aymond the gifts needed for ministry. Yet, one essential 'matter' remained void in his life.

When and how would it be filled?

Chapter 6

Two Are Better Than One

Intending to visit a young lady from Ithaca, N. Y., whom he met at Moody, Aymond 'hitched' a ride with Bethel students heading east. Previous to college years he had not felt comfortable with any girls of his acquaintance. While at Moody, he occasionally dated. Holding a firm belief that any girl, with whom he became serious, must be a Christian, proved God ordained.

When he became a student at Bethel, Aymond maintained a correspondence with the girl from New York. The relationship had become 'somewhat serious,' according to him, and thus the invitation to visit her at home.

His visit took an unexpected turn, when after two days in New York, she made it known to him she had had a change of feelings, believing they 'weren't meant for each other.' As a guest in her home, Aymond was in a predicament and thought with a sense of anguish, "This is not a good situation I'm in!" Experiencing much bewilderment, he missed his ride back to Bethel, but the former friend fortunately had a friend who bought Aymond a ticket back to Minnesota.

Commenting on this alteration of plans, Aymond said, "I am forever grateful she made this decision."

Soon, life would take a delightful new twist outside the realm of classes, extra-curricular activities, and working.

Fall always brings new students to college and that year an attractive, blond girl arrived who quickly caught Aymond's eye. Noticing her was effortless, but talking to her took courage. How could he ever ask her for a date?

The seminary laundry room with its washing machines, tubs and clotheslines, became significant. At last in this casual and somewhat homespun setting, Aymond's tongue loosened. One evening as he busily attacked his laundry, the blond, Mildred Kasen, walked in. She noticed a tall gentleman with thick brown hair, bent over the laundry tub. He looked up and greeted her with "Oh, are you the lady that washes?" Mildred knew him as a popular guy on campus. She had seen him on the Bethel stage acting out a parody of President Henry Wingblade. Assuming she was unknown to him, she replied courteously, "No, I'm sorry, I'm not." He quickly shot back at her, "Why you dirty thing," which ended the memorable introduction and forestalled further conversation. Yet the necessary courage had appeared on demand.

Later, learning about an impending school party, his former confidence in speaking to her disappeared and he debated, wondering if he dared ask her to go with him. Courage needed once again! When he learned via the grapevine another fellow planned to ask her, he dared to risk, deciding, "it's now or never, so get up your nerve now."

His confidence soared after chapel one day. Following the service he sought out Mildred and approached her saying, "I have something to say to you." Mildred claims she responded as sassy as she could muster, recalling their first meeting. Looking up at him she impudently said, "say it while your mouth is open!"

He thought he had better 'say it' without hesitation. With undiminished courage, Aymond invited her to accompany him to the Ides of March party. The perky newcomer already had a date with another young man, but that didn't stop her from saying a determined yes to Aymond. Not wasting any time, she contacted her original date that evening and told him not to pick her up for the party as she had to leave early to practice for the program.

March 13th, 1936 is a memorable day in the minds of Aymond and Mildred. Aymond walked Mildred to the school party, dumbfounded to think she had accepted his invitation. After the party they took their time walking the three blocks from school to Mildred's residence. When they arrived, she invited him in, desiring to prolong the evening. The homeowners in bed, Mildred, and Aymond sat in the living room laughing and enjoying one another. The special evening came to an end, and Aymond, not one to waste time either, kissed her goodnight. Love was on a roll!

That evening left particular memories for each of them. Mildred recalls the walk to her home, and of all things, a 'silly' mouse scurrying past them. In addition to the mouse, a life changing awareness occurred that evening, when she knew without a doubt, Aymond was the man she would someday marry!

As for Aymond? "Well, when I first saw her, really the first date, I knew this was it! I pretty much asked her to marry me that evening." Eventually, Mildred left school and went home to earn some money. "Gee," he grimaced, "it scared the wits out of me. What if I didn't get her? I still remember the dress she wore. It was maroon with a fiber cord that ended with 2 balls. I've kept the dress."

Summing it up, Aymond claims he never thought of another. He added, "The years confirmed the Lord was extremely good to me when He allowed her to come into my life."

"Our courtship was fun; fun that never ended, albeit on a meager budget," Mildred fondly recalls. She tells of one date when Aymond borrowed a fellow seminarian's car to take her to the state fair. Attempting to back out of the parking place and proceed on to get Mildred, he held the car door open for better vision. The door caught on a tree and ripped off. The friend's car door was low on his priority list of concerns. Instead, he worriedly thought 'there goes our date.' Always one to rise to the occasion, the resourceful and determined Aymond found some rope, tied the door in place, and drove to Mildred's home.

Like the popular Beverly Hillbillies the two 'Bethel hillbillies' drove to the fair in a car bound with rope. Most likely this scene caused people to stare with amazement at this peculiar sight!

The morning following another date with Mildred, Aymond stood fearfully in the office of Effie Nelson, Bethel Dean of Women! He apprehensively wondered what he had done to be called into Miss Nelson's office. He assumed any probable wrong occurred as he attempted to say goodnight to his favorite blond— (of course it was later than the rules allowed). During the good night process, he leaned on the doorbell, awakening an irate, unforgiving landlady from a sound sleep. The next morning she promptly called Miss Nelson to report such goings on. As Aymond stood waiting for the 'ax to fall,' the dean, her humor contained, told Aymond he must promise not to let it happen again. History doesn't recount what part of the promise he kept!

The romance continued in spite of deans and landladies. Mildred's parents had yet to meet her special young man. Mildred's best friend, Vangee, (the daughter of Bethel's President Wingblade), along with her parents, planned a luncheon in their home. Here Aymond could meet Mildred's parents off campus in a quiet residence. A prudent plan, but holding the possibility of a panic attack. According to Mildred, Aymond handled it superbly, impressing her parents in spite of the unusual and most likely tense setting.

Murphy's law can throw a wrench even into romantic plans. Aymond had saved his meager income so he could buy an engagement ring for Mildred. He planned to present it to Mildred on Valentine's day. Recovering at her home in Gladstone, Michigan from an appendectomy, she excitedly awaited his visit. Alas, travel plans for Aymond halted. His neck glands swelled, and the doctor's glum diagnosis confirmed a case of the Mumps! Recovery occurred, but fate seemed out to 'get him' when an inflamed appendix sent him to the hospital for his appendectomy. As soon as possible following the surgery, Aymond traveled to Mildred's home with the precious ring securely in his pocket.

As he convalesced at Mildred's home, the time had come for the romantic Aymond. At last he gave Mildred the ring he had purchased at Novak's in Minneapolis, so very long ago. She readily and happily accepted the ring and wedding plans began to soar.

In spite of a siege of puffed up glands, and minus two appendices, a 'fire-cracker wedding' took place the evening of July 4th, 1938 at Mildred's home church in Gladstone, Michigan. According to Mildred, "it was a day not even their country will let them forget."

Many relatives came from Chicago filling the home of the bride. Therefore, the only place left to dress for her wedding proved to be her dad's dental office. The bedroom which Aymond's mother and sister shared, included a closet, which remained the only private place for Aymond to put his six-foot frame into his wedding attire. In spite of the inconveniences, a handsome couple showed up at the church. Mildred wore a lovely white satin dress, trimmed with lace, tiny pearls, and sequins costing the enormous price of $18.00! Her aunt had the headpiece and veil made for Mildred. Aymond's sister Alice was Mildred's maid of honor and her cousin, Violet Kasen bridesmaid.

Aymond looked handsome in a dark coat and light pants and 'held up' beautifully, according to the bride. The groom focusing only on Mildred said, "she really looked pretty all 'fuzzed up.' Mel Kasen, Mildred's brother, served as Aymond's best man, and Herb Anderson, a mutual friend, his other attendant.

Mildred's pastor, Nils Hedstrand, performed the candlelight ceremony, but had difficulty reading the words in front of him due to the dim light of the candles. Natalie Storman Hagg, an accomplished musician, pianist at Soul's Harbor in Minneapolis and at Rex Humbard's Cathedral of Tomorrow television program as well as Mildred's mentor at the piano, added to the sacred service with her exceptional music.

A lovely reception planned by Mildred's aunt, Edith Kasen took place in the church parlors where guests greeted the newlyweds and enjoyed fruit salad (made with Knox gelatin), finger sandwiches and wedding cake. There was no such thing as RSVP in those days, so Aunt Edith needed to guess at the number of people attending.

After the reception, Aymond and Mildred left the church and climbed into her parent's car. On this romantic, moonlight night they drove to Whitefish Bay hill filled with the awesome knowledge they were now one in the sight of God.

At Mildred's home where they planned to change clothes, her brother warned them that some mischief makers planned to abduct Aymond, put him in a boat and toss him into the lake. To get the couple safely to the Ludington Hotel, eight miles away proved a challenge but Melvin met it. Knowing Aymond couldn't swim, he notified the authorities. As a result, the newlyweds had a police escort to their hotel, arriving safely. The next day suitcases in tow and sparkling rings on their fingers, Aymond and Mildred began their honeymoon in a borrowed car, setting off to tour upper Michigan.

One year later on their first wedding anniversary, Mildred took Aymond to the top of the Statue of Liberty, where she reminded him that he indeed had lost his independence!

Yes, two are better than one, but six exceeds two. Four sons eventually joined the attractive blond and tall, handsome, dark haired man. Eventually Dan, Dick, Dave, and Dennis completed the family of six. Mildred and Aymond both say, "we are so blessed."

Chapter 7

Diploma and Bible in Hand

$\mathcal{A}$ymond graduated from Bethel Seminary in 1938 following education at Moody Bible School and Bethel College and Seminary. Armed with a Bachelor of Theology degree, and a new bride at his side, he felt a sense of confidence as he embarked on a lifetime of ministry. Fathering children belonged in the unknown future. Time would prove him capable.

While earning his Theology degree, Aymond pastored part time at Lake Park Church on Como and Pascal streets near Bethel College. After graduation and marriage he was equipped to serve full time at the Lake Park Church.

The newlyweds excitedly set up their first home in the upstairs kitchenette apartment of C.E. Carlson, dean of Bethel College. The rent of $90.00 a month left $3.00 to buy meat for the following four weeks. Mrs. Carlson offered some tried and true advice to Mildred, telling her "Be sure you don't get in the habit of doing everything for your husband." She explained one method she had mastered. Thinking her husband ought to iron his own pants, she used her head as well as the iron and pressed the crease neatly on the side, rather than the center. Her ingenuity happily ended that duty.

Eventually, a request came from Bethel Baptist Church in Marinette, Wisconsin asking Aymond to become their pastor. Aymond looked upon the ministry at Lake Park church as a joyous one, but following God's nudge to head for Marinette, Aymond and Mildred decided to 'go for it.' Wedding gifts and household items packed they left the frozen Minnesota winters and began a new ministry challenge in the equally frosty Wisconsin weather.

During the pastorate in Marinette, news blared from radios across the world, reporting that the Japanese had bombed Pearl Harbor. Fear struck the hearts of Americans as the reports began to penetrate their numb minds. They knew many young men would have to give up their freedom and possibly their lives so as to provide liberty for the families left behind. Once again Aymond faced a decision about his future, contemplating whether to enter the chaplaincy for the duration of the war, or remain in the ministry where God had planted him.

In a short time, thoughts of leaving Marinette dissipated, as life in the parsonage took on a new dimension. Aymond and Mildred welcomed their first son, Dan, into their lives and home. The initial joy filling their hearts turned to a heavy weight, when they learned their baby would have to undergo years of corrective surgery due to clubfeet. During the first seven years of Dan's life, he not only had several major surgeries, but also casts and corrective devices applied to straighten his feet. This proved a sobering and testing time for Aymond and Mildred. Together they asked God to have His way in Dan's life, trusting him to an all-powerful God. These trying years challenged them emotionally and spiritually.

Aymond expressed the thoughts of parents everywhere when he said, "You know, you never expect anything to be wrong with the baby, you know." Eventually, acceptance conquered distress and the corrective efforts became part of their lives. "We had a super doctor, a super doctor and he did the final surgery." Continuing, he added emphatically, "I want to say one word about this: to see Dan now, you don't notice it."

During the years of World War II, Aymond, Mildred, and Dan moved to Wilmington, Delaware where Aymond became pastor of the Grace Baptist Church. Wilmington is located on the immense Delaware bay, which flows into the Atlantic Ocean. Here Aymond witnessed 'home front' war activity at its height as enormous naval vessels were built to aid in the war effort. He felt the joy when servicemen returned from active duty, but knew the heartache when families said farewell to loved ones leaving for overseas assignment. Pastor Aymond felt a definite burden for these boys and when those known to him were ready to leave, he counted it his privilege to be at the railroad station and pray for them.

The atmosphere of WW II contrasted from that of the First World War. At that time, an impassioned rah-rah feeling reigned among those remaining at home. The emotions of WW II failed to match the cheering level, remaining deadly serious.

Income for many on the home front came from working in war plants and building war related 'tools.' Railroad stations brimmed with tearful families bidding goodbye to loved ones who bravely attempted to mask their fear. Women went without 'necessities' such as nylon hosiery, intent on doing their 'bit' for the boys. Due to gas rationing, the family car was driven only when necessary. Men kept the car tires patched as well as their shoes. Rarely could others be purchased. The school children did their part by saving pennies and nickels to buy war bonds.

At the Grace Baptist Church, Pastor Aymond made certain the service men and women were honored. During each evening service, a spotlight illuminated the American flag, which gently rippled with the aid of a large fan. The congregation joined together in singing their theme chorus:

"God bless our boys, wherever they may be,
Upon the land, or on the rolling sea,
Or in the air, we follow them with prayer
God bless our boys, God bless our boys.
God bless you every one,
God bless you in our prayers,

God bless you and keep you,
In His loving care."

Often service men or women who came to the church services felt honored by an invitation to the parsonage. There they
enjoyed a homey atmosphere as they relished Mildred's 'yummy'
goodies and the enjoyment of an evening in this special home.
They left aware they were prayed for and cared about.

Like most committed pastors, Aymond kept a demanding
schedule. In addition to his already brimful schedule, high medical bills created the need to supplement his clergy income. The
shipyard met that need as they hired him as a guard from 11:00
P.M. to 7:00 A.M. every night. During the day, he somehow managed to fulfill his pastoral duties.

The Wilmington church granted Aymond permission to conduct evangelistic meetings in other churches each spring and
fall, His gift for evangelism began to bloom while in seminary
and the invitations continued after graduation. Because of this
he requested from each pastorate a leave of absence twice a year.
He continued doing this for thirty years, some meetings lasting
two weeks (including three Sundays), others, eight great days,
and some a long weekend (Wed. through Sunday).

In spite of his day and night agenda, Aymond agreed to speak
at meetings in Bristol, Connecticut for one week. He describes
his unbelievable timetable previous to the 'eight great days' in
Bristol: "I came home from guard duty after 7:00 A.M. on a Sunday morning, taught Sunday School and preached at 11:00 A.M.
I then took a train to Bristol where I spoke at their evening service. I couldn't sleep on the train as it was crawling with servicemen."

He continued, "No, but I had an interesting experience on
the train. The seats faced each other and I sat with four servicemen. One especially was dead drunk. As the men approached
their destination, the others in an attempt to awaken the intoxicated man pinched him and pressed his eyeballs. Nothing worked
and he had to be carried off. I never knew what happened to

him, but just think," Aymond commented with compassion, "he was someone's son! Lots of heartaches."

After speaking that same Sunday evening at the church service, he at last could give his body some rest, and claimed, "I finally went to my hotel and to bed, not having slept for 24 hours." Nevertheless, lack of sleep didn't hinder his effectiveness and he considered the meetings as 'a source of inspiration.'

Mildred remembers Aymond coming home from these meetings refreshed and feeling fulfilled. "He regularly featured kids," she relates. "As he talked to them, they sat fascinated; their eyes glued to his flat thumb waving before them while gesturing emphatically. Even in later years these now grown children have come to him recounting they had accepted Christ while being in his booster club."

During his Wilmington ministry, Aymond faced the evils and tragedy's resulting from alcohol use.

Early one evening he stepped out the front door to retrieve his newspaper thrown on the porch. The darkening sky hindered his vision, yet he noticed some unusual and curious activity across the street.

A dark shape moved slowly along the sidewalk, then disappeared, eventually reappearing. This odd scene continued to be repeated. Curiosity aroused, Aymond walked closer so as to see clearly and have his inquisitive mind satisfied. The shadowy object which kept vanishing proved to be a nine year old boy who periodically fell, followed by a difficult struggle to get back on his feet. The heartbreaking reason? He was attempting to carry his intoxicated father home!

Every month pastor and people from the Wilmington church traveled to the city 'rescue' mission on skid row. Bent on a mission with a purpose they presented the gospel in song, testimonies of what Christ had accomplished in their lives, and preaching by Aymond. 'Old Joe,' one of the transients always showed up wearing a long black coat with one sleeve-hanging limp, as a result of having his arm severed at the wrist.

One day on his way to speak at a Christian businessmen's luncheon meeting, Aymond stopped at a delicatessen. Who should walk in, but 'old Joe.' Aymond expected Joe would be asked to leave. Instead, Joe walked to the counter and mumbled to the waitress, "I want my money." Frank, the owner immediately went to the register and took out $15.00 and without hesitation gave it to Joe.

After Joe left and Frank returned to his office, Aymond inquired of the waitress about the incident. She told him, "One time old Joe was one of the best dressed men in Wilmington and owned this building. But he began to drink and lost everything. Frank, who had bought the building from Joe, felt so sorry for him, that he promised to give him $15.00 a month as long as Joe lived."

Ministry at the mission, pastoring his congregation and preaching at special meetings for other churches, plus working at night to pay off extra expenses, seems humanly impossible to achieve. Yet, God provided strength for Aymond and a perfect helper for him. Mildred enabled him to carry out his ministry as well as his 'other' job. She ministered faithfully using her talents in the church, as well as at home being wife, mother, housekeeper, and hostess. Obviously this left scant amount of time for rest. Many lonely days and evenings were spent even though filled with mothering Dan and eventually a second son Dick, who arrived during the ministry in Wilmington. After four 'chock-full' years at the Grace Church another church beckoned Aymond to become their pastor.

Aymond knew God was leading him to the ministry of First Baptist Church of Sister Bay, Wisconsin. As he prepared to leave Wilmington, word came that World War II had ended! With joy and much relief masses of people swarmed the streets, celebrating this long awaited victory. He not only bid his church family farewell, but also Mildred and their two boys. Unfortunately, traveling together proved impossible, as Mildred and the boys had to remain behind and wait for their ordered automobile to arrive. Production on cars began after the end of the war, and due to the demand delivery was agonizingly slow. Several months later, the car arrived and Mildred with two little boys drove the many miles alone to Sister Bay and finally the family was together again.

During the nine years Aymond pastored in Sister Bay, their family unit grew with the addition of two little boys, David, and Dennis. Aymond remembers a woman from the church telling him, "I think you now have enough children." Asked how he responded, he claims he didn't answer her, as "it was none of her business!" In the fish bowl existence of a pastor and family the grace of God is essential!

Not surprising, an imposing schedule awaited him in Sister Bay. At the time, First Baptist Church held the largest membership in the conference district. The expectations for pastor and wife loomed enormous, attempting to overshadow family life. 'In charge of all things' could simplify the 'job description' in that era. The expected duties of the pastor, included responsibility for the youth programs along with other expectations.

Mildred assumed all secretarial work, together with typing and printing the weekly bulletins. Antiquated mimeograph machines helped elevate the frustration level each week. The secretaries at that time, (either pastor or wife) first had to take a blue stencil and type the information with a heavy hand in order to cut through the thickness. Then ink was poured into the drum of the mimeograph and the stencil was laid on top of the gelatinous surface. Finally, it was time to stand and turn the crank until enough bulletins etc. were produced. Hopefully, they looked presentable, but the hands of the secretary needed washing to remove the blue ink.

The beauty of the area the family called home transcended any daily inconveniences. A short distance traveling either east or west on the peninsula brought the sight of the relaxing waters of Green Bay and Lake Michigan. Sand beaches and high rocky cliffs seemed to guard the waters. Beyond the beaches and high on the cliffs, towering evergreens stood wearing shades of green throughout the seasons which contrasted to the incredibly beautiful, stately, white birch. When the Maple trees displayed their fall beauty, the scene seemed complete, all painted by the Lord Aymond and Mildred served.

Not to be outdone, groves of cherry trees burst into masses of white blossoms in the spring, yielding to clusters of ruby, red cherries which in mid-summer hung heavily from the tree branches. Thousands of migrant workers arrived by truck to pick the luscious fruit, readying them for market. Indians and Mexicans, along with southern blacks and local families, were among those who aided in the harvest. The plentiful cherries were all plucked by hand, as mechanical picking machines had not yet been constructed. Pastor Aymond, Mildred, and their boys were among the pickers and often many cherries ended in Mildred's scrumptious pies.

Tents were provided for the migrant workers to temporarily live in. In these camps, First Baptist Church saw a ready ministry and formed gospel teams that held services for the workers. Recordings of Spanish music on small wind-up players and preaching often by Aymond told the gospel story. The four Anderson children didn't complain about attending the services, but they did not relish picking cherries. Aymond observed, "It was a good ministry. Who knows if they became Christians or not; at least the congregation cared enough to get involved."

As a result, many of the migrant pickers came to the Sunday services at First Baptist. One Sunday morning prior to the service, Aymond took his place on the platform. While waiting for the organist to finish her prelude, he looked over the congregation and observed a man walking down the aisle. Aymond knew there weren't any seats available up front, but not to worry, the man strode to the platform and sat in the chair beside Aymond.

Leaning towards Aymond, he announced, "I'm going to preach this morning." As Aymond concealed his astonishment, he most likely sent up an SOS prayer. Equipped with a dose of wisdom from the Lord, he responded to his unexpected platform visitor by saying, "The service is well planned, but we have a service on Wed. evening, and we would be happy to have you speak then." Satisfied, the man quietly found a seat in the audience. The visitor turned out to be a 'no-show' the next Wed., but Aymond claims he would have allowed him to speak.

Pastors generally are not expecting an effervescent response to their sermons or prayers. Yet, one Sunday morning in the predominately Swedish origin, white skinned, Sister Bay church, the unexpected occurred. The sanctuary overflowed and the ushers needed to place chairs in every possible area, even directly in front of the pulpit. Here, in the extreme front, sat a row of visiting cherry pickers.

The congregation stood to sing the first hymn, and remained standing while Aymond prayed. With eyes closed, he concluded the opening prayer. Suddenly, a very tall man standing squarely in front of Aymond thundered "AMEN!" The startled preacher gripped the pulpit, while the Swedes in the congregation held their breath and dead silence momentarily prevailed. The pastor's heart rate returned to normal, the congregation breathed a sigh of relief as the unexpected became accepted.

In addition to unannounced platform visitors and loud amen's, the 'unexpected' can come in the form of non-human competition.

It was time for the sermon. As Aymond began speaking, he noticed a movement out of the corner of his eye. He turned and to his surprise saw the family kitten had come to church, choosing the platform as its pew. Aymond knew the audience's attention would center on the kitty if he tried to ignore it. Cats claim the reputation of being uncooperative, so Aymond reasoned, if he tried to pick him up, who knows where the kitty might run to; possibly under the pews or partake in unimaginable activity that could really disrupt the service. "Wouldn't it be a circus to see the preacher chasing a cat around the church?" he thought. "Instead I went up to the cat and said 'here kitty, kitty!' The cat arched his back and let me pick him up." As he put the cat into a side room, the congregation smiled at the unexpected entertainment that Sunday morning, a prelude to Sunday dinner conversations and laughter.

Distinct from the unexpected, choral and instrumental groups blessed the Sister Bay congregation. Under the direction of Melvin Kasen, Mildred's brother, the church became well known for its musical programs. The male chorus, (active for many years), was so revered, they were invited to sing at the Chicago music festival; indeed an honor.

Christians as well as non-believers entered the doors of the Sister Bay Church for Sunday services. One Christian mother attended, occasionally accompanied by her son Carl, who like his dad did not profess the Christian faith. Mother and son attended the Sunday evening service when Pastor Aymond preached from II Kings 6:24. Speaking on "The Man with the Secret Care," he reminded the congregation how we respond to the question 'how are you?' and the answer usually is, 'just fine.' In doing so, we lock our cares behind the bars of our inner prison. Pastor Aymond prompted the congregation to think of other secrets that they carry including the serious, secret sin of never accepting Jesus as Savior.

The next day the office phone rang. When Aymond answered it, he heard the excited voice of a woman saying, "I can't believe it! Carl has been saved! Carl has been saved!" Subsequently, Carl related his story to Aymond. "Last night in church, I was the one with the secret care. Today, in the orchard as I pruned the cherry trees, the burden I carried became heavier and heavier. Finally, I dropped to my knees and cried out to Jesus asking Him to save me." With thanksgiving he said, "It felt as though I had been wearing a heavy winter coat and now it was gone!" Praise God!

A strong believer in friendship evangelism, Aymond won many to Christ through his preaching, but also using his unique, God given philosophy when he shared Christ personally with others: "they've got to feel comfortable. The condition of their soul is very private to them. People won't hand that out to just anybody."

At the request of an individual from his congregation, Aymond visited a wealthy, older man in his home. Known for his cynical and extremely bitter attitudes, he successfully locked people out of his life. Following up on the request, Aymond visited him, armed with Mildred's rice pudding and minus a Bible or plan to pray. Following subsequent visits, Aymond asked if it would be all right if he prayed and was told, "If it makes you feel better, go ahead." Eventually, hospitalization for this man changed the locale for visits. As Aymond walked into his hospital room, the patient asked Aymond to light the cigarette hanging from his mouth. Aymond complied while thinking, "What if the church people could see me now?" When he finished the task, the patient told Aymond, "You're a good kid!"

When visiting the man at a later time, Aymond said to him, "Whether you believe it or not God loves you." At this, he began to cry and said, "I'm glad somebody does." Aymond knowing he wasn't as hard as he pretended seized the opportunity. He said to him, "I'm going to tell you how you can be saved. I don't have to be here when you pray, but I'll tell you how. Pray like this: Lord Jesus I know I'm a sinner." At these words, Aymond wondered if his ears deceived him when he heard him repeat his words in prayer. During that hospital visit one more individual exchanged his hardened heart for a new life in Jesus Christ!

When Aymond left the room and stood outside the hospital, he shouted out loud, "Lord, I can't believe it!" At another visit, he saw the man smile for the first time, and heard him say, "I was looking for you." The power of friendship evangelism!

Following his full-time years of pastoring, Aymond sat in the dining room of his Ellison Bay home and reflected on these years. He talked of a time when his attitude toward people changed and the positive effect it had on his ministry. "When I began my ministry, I don't feel I had a real love for the people. It became easy for me to be quite judgmental." During the Sister Bay pastorate, he preached a message on Christian love. That effective sermon evolved into a series of 14 messages. Aymond felt he was the one who benefited the most, as "it really changed my ministry. I learned how foolish it was to judge people."

As Aymond preached through the series, God used an incident that helped change his attitude. The family of a non-Christian husband attended the church. He became ill and subsequently was hospitalized. Knowing the man, Aymond's thinking about him had centered on, "You'll get yours someday!" As a result, love and compassion failed to accompany Aymond when he visited him in the hospital. Yet, as Aymond visited with him, the man suddenly began to cry and said, "I can't believe in a God who took my Dad away when I was a little boy." Aymond feeling guilty thought, "I have been so stupid. I should have loved him." Later the two became friends and the man put his faith in Christ, knowing God did indeed love him.

During their pastorate in Sister Bay, Aymond and Mildred made a decision that played a significant role in their lives. Loving the beautiful Door County area, they purchased a lot on the Green Bay shore where Aymond used his many skills and eventually built a small 16 x 30 cottage. A generous church member offered the needed trees from his forty acres. God provided for Mildred and Aymond through His servant, but Aymond had to supply the muscle power. He cut every tree with a handsaw. "No chain saws on the scene yet," he reminisced. When the trees were all cut, Aymond hauled them to the mill where they were planed into finished lumber. Conscientious Aymond built the cottage late at night, so as not to take away from his pastoral duties, working from 10:00 P.M. until 2:00 A.M.

The family loved their cottage and the surrounding area so much that when they eventually moved from Sister Bay, they returned every summer for a one-month vacation. The boys love for the area was evidenced by Dennis' response when given a choice of Disney Land or Sister Bay. He chose a vacation in their beloved Sister Bay cottage. Eventually Aymond added a 10 x 12 sunroom addition and a deck to their cottage.

Yet while still residents of Sister Bay, Aymond experienced what he called a 'bad year.' The misery began when he took one of his famous falls. Following the evening service, he ran out of church, hurrying to keep an invitation for 'after church coffee and goodies.' In his haste, he slipped on a piece of ice and in doing so, threw his arms backward to break the fall. Assuming he had escaped injury, he continued on his way. It took two weeks before discomforts made an appearance and he felt a little sting in both arms. The sting quickly emerged into acute pain, became progressively worse, spreading throughout his body. "It got so bad, I couldn't do anything—even turn the key in the car, and of course I couldn't drive" he recalled. "I became almost helpless; Mildred even had to dress me. Eating was painful and I couldn't open my mouth wide enough to eat a hamburger without taking it apart.

"Then came doctors—even a 'voodoo' who gave me large doses of muscle relaxants, which would have killed me if another doctor had not obtained my release from the hospital. Finally, I went to the Mayo Clinic and after all the tests, they concluded I had tendonitis in every tendon of my body. The cure—just leave it alone and rest. I continued pastoring during this time, missing only two Sundays, but it took a year before it improved."

Following this 'bad' year Mildred and Aymond made the painful decision to put their cottage on the market. Years later, he gratefully commented, "We wouldn't have the farm we now own if we hadn't sold the cottage." Selling this loved place in their family life, became confirmed eventually, when a faithful God Who remembers, opened the door for Aymond to own another farm.

After eight years of pastoring the Sister Bay church, the time came when Mildred and Aymond felt led to leave this ministry for another opportunity. The church held a farewell for their beloved pastor and family. Unknown to many, Aymond had quietly helped those in need with gifts of money as he visited in their homes. At this meaningful yet difficult occasion, many people from outside the church surprised Aymond and Mildred as they arrived from surrounding areas to say their good-byes, proving that the Anderson's had truly been a genuine blessing to people not only in the First Baptist Church, but grateful outsiders as well.

Chapter 8

God's Detour

$\mathcal{I}$will instruct you and teach you in the way you should go, I will guide you with my eye. Psalm 32:8, Aymond's life verse, evolved into a scripture that repeatedly showed God's faithfulness and direction in his life.

A missed flight to Muskegon, Michigan created a detour in Aymond's plans. He intended to candidate at the Lakeside Baptist Church in that city, but heavy traffic caused a delay in arriving at the airport, yet conceded to a fulfillment of God's plan.

Shortly after this obstacle in Aymond's plans, God in His wisdom led him to accept a call to pastor the Addison Baptist Church in Chicago, formerly the First Swedish Baptist Church. After eight years of a rewarding pastorate in Sister Bay, Mildred once again packed up the family possessions (comprised now of six people) and they moved to the metropolis of Chicago. Aymond remembers walking in downtown Chicago, reliving the time he first came to this "big, rough and tough city, green from the farm"; amazed God had placed him there again.

Church needs and major decisions awaited the new pastor. The congregation urgently needed God appointed leadership, having experienced the loss of young members who moved to the northern suburbs and formed the Skokie Valley Baptist

Church. The majority of those who left Addison had comprised the choir, contributing to a void that needed filling in the music ministry of the church.

The Addison church had 'given birth' to seventeen new churches, including the Skokie Church prior to Aymond's ministry. When Aymond began as pastor, this mother church had as an agenda to give the new Skokie church $2000.00. The congregation reacted rigorously to the idea, expressing 'let them pay their own bills.' Aymond quietly said to the people, "I sense there are some hard feelings here. If that is true, let's give them $4000.00! Boy, they voted that $2000.00 in so quick." Suggesting he used some good psychology, Aymond replied with a grin, "No, I didn't know any better. They probably thought, here's that goon up in front, what's he going to do next?"

Years later, while seated at the dining room table in his Ellison Bay home, he declared with typical forthrightness and firm voice, "Now, I'm going to tell you something. Christian love is the essence! If people give you a hard time, treat them special. It works. I cannot name one person in my ministry who gave me a hard time." He dearly loved his people and they responded to that love.

Once again, God supplied and the music ministry gap filled when Mildred's brother Melvin became music director at the Addison church. Confirming God's faithfulness, the church soon embraced a choir of 75 voices. One memorable Christmas, the choir sang inspiring portions of the beloved Messiah, assisted by the Nordic symphony ensemble.

The Lord blessed this congregation and its pastor. Every Sunday morning Aymond gave a brief invitation at the close of his message. "Almost, without exception, always, always," he said with great emphasis, "people responded to the invitation and received Christ as their Savior. I remember hundreds between the Denver church and Addison!"

He felt it important for people to become accustomed to the idea of going forward, making their decision public. Many who responded to the invitation on Sunday morning had accepted Christ in their home. Numerous evenings Aymond visited in homes, often going into areas of violence. He built a rapport with the families, which frequently led to conversing about their spiritual lives. Their need to feel comfortable with him ruled out a one-time visit. He wanted them to know him as a personal friend, not merely a professional doing his 'job.' At times it took years to accomplish his goal.

He told each person who had become a Christian an invitation would be given at the conclusion of his message the following Sunday and requested them to respond. As they witnessed others 'walking the aisle' they had the courage to make an open declaration of their newfound faith. This also gave others the courage to 'walk the aisle.'

As usual one Sunday morning, Aymond gave an invitation for people to receive Christ as Savior. A young man by the name of Joe spoke to Aymond as he left the church saying, "I really felt this was the time for me," but he had not come forward in response to the invitation. Aymond talked to him a few days later about their conversation. He asked Joe if he would like to give his life to Christ now. Joe replied, "I don't feel like that any more." "How sad," Aymond commented, "in light of 'Today is the day of salvation; now is the accepted time.' (II Corinthians 6:2) Joe did not think it important to take advantage of his 'to-day.'"

A contrast in attitude was noted when the same invitation was given another Sunday. While waiting for people to decide if they should embrace Christ's way of life, he noticed a young woman seated in the balcony. She responded by raising her hand, then turned, and kissed her boyfriend prior to walking to the front of the sanctuary. It appeared to Aymond that she said to her friend, "I'm going with Christ even though it means goodbye."

As people became Christians and the congregation increased in numbers, Aymond needed staff to assist him in this active ministry. In addition to Melvin Kasen working with the music program, he tells how fortunate he was to have a young man who had grown up in the church as his youth pastor. "George Rice was deeply committed to youth, which evidenced itself in the 45–50 high school kids attending camp each summer. The church became number one in church league athletics—mainly softball and basketball," Aymond concluded with a sense of pride.

During the week, Aymond kept a demanding schedule leaving little time at home with his family. His day began in the office at 8:00 A.M., studying in preparation for Sunday services and other speaking opportunities. After lunch he climbed in the car and called on people not only in their homes, but visited those hospitalized. In the Chicago area this meant spending much time driving long distances between hospitals and fighting heavy traffic. Most of his evenings overflowed with board meetings or home visitation. Wisely, Mildred and Aymond kept Monday for themselves, free from church activities. Mildred recalls Chicago as "one place we really had a day together." They often played golf on the Evanston course, not because of their ability, but for fun. Although she added, "Aymond couldn't have been too bad as he has made two holes in one during his playing years."

In addition to golf, they loved to go 'bumming.' A favorite haunt became the Maxwell St. shopping area dominated by Jewish merchants noted for being very shrewd in bargaining. As they walked along the streets, peering into the shops and haggling with shopkeepers, it seemed as though they had landed in a foreign land. Wearing clothes from shops on Maxwell Street, he asked a friend to guess the amount of money he spent on these clothes. For his suit, shirt, tie and shoes he had paid the unbelievable sum of $22.50.

A favorite merchant on Maxwell Street was a Jewish man named Kelly who featured sporting goods in his shop where the Addison Street Church purchased their sporting equipment. "Oh, that was such an interesting place," Aymond reminisced. "I'd always ask Kelly if I should go 'over there' to buy a hat or something and he'd reply, 'they'll try to hook you, you know. They drive a hard bargain and you won't be able to make the best deal.' Aymond and Mildred felt they knew Kelly so well, that when son Dick was married they invited him to the wedding. Kelly later commented, "I can't believe how much fun they had without any drinking."

Relaxing 'fun' proved a diversion from Aymond's hectic ministry schedule, yet occasionally ended with an unexpected adventure. One day he and a friend walked in the woods intent on cutting a downed tree.

A gigantic tree had blown down leaving a massive root section attached. The men planned to saw the tree into three lengths. As the friend began sawing at the top end, Aymond stood on the tree close to the top thinking his weight could keep the tree positioned. The instant the saw cut into the wood, the immense root system caused the tree to do the unexpected.

"Suddenly the tree made a sound like 'yip, yip, yip,' and sprang upright," according to Aymond. As he fell off his stance near the treetop and landed on another log lying nearby, he felt convinced he was about to meet his Maker. Knowing he could move his legs, his friend assumed he wasn't injured. Aymond then climbed down a 30-foot cliff and drove home unaware he had fractured his back. His 'relaxing' day turned into a painful one including admittance to the hospital and the application of a steel brace. Who knows what became of the hoped for logs, but Aymond, the tough woodsman, missed only two Sundays of preaching.

Having fun and exercise became a needed benefit physically, and produced an emotional lift that helped ease the demands of ministry. At times the responsibilities seem overwhelming to a pastor. Such a somber time occurred within the life of Addison Church. A young man who attended Sunday School at the church had gone to a local park. Also in the park was a police officer under the influence of alcohol.

For an unknown reason he shot and killed the young man. "I had the funeral and it was a sad, sad time," Aymond soberly recalled. In the midst of these sorrowful events, a pastor as well as congregation is plunged into the crisis, not understanding the 'why,' but trusting that God is in control.

Occasionally the deceased and their families are unknown to a pastor. At one such funeral Aymond arrived and found only one mourner present; the brother of the deceased. Waiting for the service to begin, he thought, "Am I going to stand behind the pulpit and preach only to him?" Yet, he felt deeply saddened for this man, so alone. Instead of the planned sermon, Aymond left his chair, and sat down beside the man and placed his arm around his shoulders. The sermon went unpreached, but as Aymond talked and prayed with him, the man sensed Christ's compassion through Aymond's loving comfort. This man began attending Addison church; brought by love and remained because of love. He never missed a Sunday and Aymond felt he had made a decision for Christ.

Showing compassion for one man at a funeral, contrasts with the thousands of people at a Billy Graham crusade held in Chicago. During Aymond's pastorate he helped counsel those who responded to the invitation to accept Christ as Savior. A vast difference in numbers, but Aymond considered both experiences highly significant in his ministry.

Following the Graham crusade, Aymond visited people in the vicinity of Addison Church who had made decisions to follow Christ. This presented a challenge that resulted in thirty people who united with Addison Church. One unforgettable call occurred. "I introduced myself to the man who came to the door, telling him I understood he had made a decision for Christ." The man replied, "Not really. I went forward because I wanted to get a close look at Billy Graham!"

Pastor Aymond and the church board wanted a motto for Addison Church to remind all from the congregation and those who entered the church doors the purpose of their ministry. They chose the phrase, "Only one life, 'twill soon be past, only what's done for Christ will last." This was printed on pencils, letterheads, bulletins, and Aymond's calling cards, becoming a constant counsel to him as well as maintaining an overall impact on the ministry of the church.

A sequel to this story occurred after Aymond moved from his Chicago pastorate to Denver, CO. He received a call in the Denver office, telling about a man whose body had been found floating in the Cherry Creek reservoir near Denver. The only information in his pockets turned out to be Aymond's calling card. Aymond remembered the man had attended the church services, but when he attempted to visit him, no one was at home so he left his card printed with the church motto and his name. After receiving the sad phone call, Aymond pondered what this man had learned when he heard the gospel that day. "Only one life 'twill soon be past, Only what's done for Christ will last."

More and more the power of God's love began to manifest itself in Aymond's life. One day while driving to church on Lincoln Avenue in Chicago, he stopped for a red light and waited while a policeman escorted school children across the street. The gray-haired officer limped slightly as he walked and appeared so weary. Aymond felt a rush of compassion for him and prayed, "Lord, you see how tired he looks, help him to have a better day."

The light turned green and Aymond proceeded to cross the street just as a man began to walk across from the left. Aymond stopped the car and the man stopped walking. They repeated this scene twice, and finally as Aymond noted traffic lining up behind him, decided to drive across the intersection.

Suddenly, he heard a whistle blow. The officer observing the 'cat and mouse' game between Aymond the driver, and the pedestrian, showed his disapproval and directed Aymond to pull over.

Fuming to himself, Aymond grumbled, "Here I prayed for you, now you're going to give me a ticket." The policeman, instead gave Aymond a pedestrian's rights lecture. As he 'preached' he rested his arm on the window ledge. Finished with the reprimand, he turned to leave when Aymond with a renewed attitude, placed his hand on the officer's arm. He told him he observed how tired he looked and exactly how he had prayed for him. The officer responded with tears in his eyes, "You did that and I bawled you out as I did." Aymond left knowing the policeman had a better day because he knew someone cared for him.

Yet, at other times, those seated in the church congregation had reason to wonder how their pastor might handle an unexpected situation. Such was the case when Aymond preached at a newly organized church. He noticed a woman walking down the aisle towards him. He assumed she needed to use the ladies room; instead she stopped about three feet in front of him. There she stood, staring at him for two or three minutes. As suddenly as she appeared, she turned and left. What did Pastor Aymond do? The unflappable speaker just kept on preaching!

Many endearing experiences saturated Aymond and Mildred's ministry at Addison. Mildred's gift of hospitality consistently reached out to many grateful people. Together, pastor and wife extended love and encouragement to people in their home. Wrigley Field, the home of the Cubs, was only two blocks away from the church and the ball players often attended services. On a Sunday evening the players and their wives benefited from a warm welcome in Mildred and Aymond's home. After one occasion in the Anderson home, a note came from the pitcher's wife, Mrs. Johnny Buzzhart. Following her thank you, she added, "There is so much sorrow in a baseball players life." Aymond summed this up when he remarked, "All is not glitter . . ."

Aymond's sermons were often peppered with stories about people. One especially he loved to tell, was a remarkable story about two transformed lives. One was the story of Jacob De Shazer who respected his Christian parents, (his father a pastor and farmer) but chose not to agree with their faith. As a result he decided it best to leave home and join the service. Then came Pearl Harbor. In great anger Jacob boasted, "Just wait until we take care of those blankety, blank Japs."

Days went on. Eventually an invitation came to volunteer for a secret and dangerous mission to bomb Tokyo under the command of Jimmy Dolittle. Jacob's squadron was the first to leave to ready for this mission and his plane #16, was the final one to leave the carrier. After the bombing run was completed the plane headed back for the carrier. On the way, Jacob saw a Japanese fishing boat and unleashing his anger, he fired on it. His plane soon ran out of gas and following a forced landing he was taken prisoner by the Japanese.

Normally his actions could have resulted in execution as a war criminal, but God had other plans for him. As he sat in his cell, bored and with nothing to occupy his mind except thoughts of his past life and his Christian parents, he asked for a Bible and received it. While reading the scriptures the Holy Spirit opened his heart as he came face to face with his spiritual need. Jacob repented of his sins and joyfully gave his life to Christ. As a new Christian, Jacob's attitude became transformed and the hatred formerly held towards the Japanese no longer overpowered him. The next morning following his conversion, Jacob said a pleasant 'good morning' to the guard, much to the watchman's amazement. An improved change in their relationship between prisoner and guard began to take place. As a result, the guard brought Jacob special items he would not ordinarily receive, such as a boiled potato. As Jacob spent time alone in prison, he took the opportunity to ponder his future. Desiring to serve his God he determined when released from prison, he would return to the states and come back to Japan as a missionary. His testimony would eventually influence the Japanese Fleet commander, Mitsuo Fuchida, whom Aymond would meet at Addison Church.

Following WW II, Aymond read in a periodical about a man who had commanded a fleet of 360 Japanese bombers that had bombed Pearl Harbor on that horrendous day of Dec. 7th, 1941. This man was Mitsuo Fuchida, and as Aymond read he learned that Mitsuo had given his life to Christ. Mitsuo convinced the Japanese were justified, firmly believed in the war, yet his life had been miraculously spared on several occasions. Subsequently, following the horrible Atomic bomb explosion, he experienced increasing despondency and his life began to lack meaning. One day he sat dejectedly on a curb in Tokyo. A member of the Pocket Testament League passed by and seeing this sad appearing man, he reached into his pocket and chose a tract to give him. The tract's title, "I Was A War Prisoner in Japan" by Jacob DeShazer.

Mitsuo had noticed the compassionate actions of a young girl while working with war prisoners. When he asked her why she treated them so kindly, she replied, "My parents were killed by the Japanese." She then told him how her parents, prior to their assassination, had asked their captors to allow them a half an hour to pray, that they might ask God to forgive their captors. As a result of a young girl's compassion towards those she had reason to hate and the tract he received, this Japanese commander turned his life over to Christ. Mitsuo's heart had found what he needed in Christ. He subsequently authored a book titled "From Pearl Harbor to Golgotha."

Eventually he teamed up with Elmer Sacs to form a boys program entitled Sky Pilots, and visited the United States to promote it. Aymond met Mitsuo when he shared his story at the Addison church and received his book "From Pearl Harbor to Golgotha." Aymond's impression of Mitsuo was of a man very small in stature, yet possessing an immense faith.

If a stranger observed Aymond as he made home and hospital calls they would not suspect what he was 'up to.' He didn't wear a clerical (backwards) collar (being a Baptist) and he didn't carry a Bible (even though a Baptist). His philosophy was and is, down to earth. "Many people are uncomfortable in the presence of preachers," maintains Aymond. "I have a small Bible in my pocket when I visit the first few times. We have a friendly chat—no Bible reading or prayer. When they are comfortable with me things can change."

Such was the hospital call he made to the father of a young woman from Addison. The father told his daughter, "Now don't send any preacher to see me," but in spite of the request, she felt right in requesting Aymond to visit. After several amicable visits with Carl, Aymond said, "I want to talk to you about something. Just then Carl's lunch tray came and Aymond decided he should leave. Soon Carl returned home. When Aymond walked into the house, Carl reminded him that he wanted to talk about a certain matter. Aymond sensing a perfect opening explained the plan of salvation to Carl. That day, Carl readily received Christ as his Savior. Shortly, his condition worsened and the final visit took place at Cook County Hospital, where his last words to Aymond were "He forgave all of my sin."

There are many that claim eternal life with Christ, as a result of Aymond and Mildred's ministry. A member of Addison, C. George Erickson, wrote the history of the church for the 100th anniversary. Also editor at that time of the Baptist General Conference magazine, "The Standard" he had experienced the Anderson's effective pastorate. He commented in his writing, "While Mildred and Aymond were at Addison, their ministry was characterized by Christian love." Aymond's response to this was a joyful, "Could anything be greater? If people know you really love them they will gladly allow anything."

Aymond feels too many pastors think their 'job' is to rule over the people. The treasurer of International Harvester was a member at Addison. Aymond referred to him as a 'big guy,' who was one of a number of businessmen in the congregation. So Aymond figured, "Let them run the church. I'll do what I can do," and he added, "it works!" As a result, people respected Aymond's God given wisdom. When the need arose to increase space in the church basement and add folding doors, this caused financial worries. As a result, the priority question became, "What does Aymond think?" When the answer was 'he's for it,' the congregation pursued the remodeling project, demonstrating their regard and love for a humble pastor.

Aymond claims he hasn't encountered the inner pain many people have had to endure. Yet, he is not embarrassed at shedding tears over their distress. One day before entering a fast food place for a bite of lunch, he looked around the corner and saw an older man sitting on the ground eating. The sight of this pathetic appearing man, so lonely and alone, brought tears to Aymond's eyes. Another time, he noticed a poorly dressed man searching through a dumpster hoping to find food. As the man began to leave, Aymond felt compelled to give him money and ran after him. "Even though some would say, 'he will only spend it on liquor,' mine is to give if God urges me to do so." He concludes, "If he spends it on drink, that is his problem, my responsibility is to show compassion."

This expanding compassion for people throughout his ministry, became the essence of Aymond's life as his ministry to others in Jesus name continued.

Aymond and three
sisters - 1908

The Anderson family - Mr. and Mrs. Anderson, Aymond and four
sisters - 1910.

Aymond's early farming years. Leaning on a pitchfork at 10 years of age.

When a Moody student in Chicago, his training included ministering in a prison. Late 1920's.

Aymond, a Bethel College/
Seminary student.
1934–1938.

Mildred and Aymond bride and groom on July 4th, 1937.

Mildred and Aymond's four boys -
Dick, Dennis, David, and Dan.

Aymond, Mildred and four boys - 1959

Aymond pastor of
Immanuel Baptist Church,
Denver, CO.

Cherry picking time in Door County, WI. Aymond picked over 100
pails a day. Approximately 1945.

"Friendly Acres," Mildred and Aymond's home in Ellison Bay, WI.

Mildred and Aymond celebrate 65 years of marriage in 2002.

Dr. George Brushaber president of Bethel University and Bethel Seminary presented Aymond with the distinguished Medal of Honor in 2001. In May of 2004, Dr. Brushaber presented Aymond with a picture of Bethel's beautiful campus, and also surprised him with the news that a wing of one of the buildings would be dedicated in his honor. The inscription reads: Rev. Aymond Anderson College class of 1936 Seminary class of 1938.

Chapter 9

A Brief View of the Mountains

When a pastor and wife bids a beloved congregation farewell, it can be a heart wrenching experience even though they know an inner certainty of God's plan for them. Therefore, out of necessity, the endless stack of boxes begin to fill in the midst of conflicting emotions.

Following eight years of ministry at the Addison Church in Chicago Mildred and Aymond, obedient to God's leading, began a new and challenging pastorate at the Immanuel Baptist Church of Denver, Colorado. Their years in the mile high city would prove enjoyable, but brief.

The spiritual rewards of this new pastorate evidenced itself as the attendance increased and many accepted Christ as their Savior. The church's prime ministry to young adults attracted 50 young people to the college class and 60 into the career age group. This group loved to receive invitations to Mildred and Aymond's home, and they in turn welcomed them lovingly into their home.

As with most people in ministry, Aymond and Mildred experienced the mountaintop moments where the sun appears to shine brighter, the bird's singing brings a sense of joy, and 'all seems right with the world.' In contrast, when no rewards are evident, and a crisis befalls a church family, they share the pain, often precluding all else.

On one occasion Aymond was called to the hospital to visit a young man. Aymond marveled at the shortness of the boy's body. He learned that two brothers had been rabbit hunting. One of the brothers explained to Aymond, "We were driving in a new Jeep, but when it began snowing we decided to head home. As we turned around, the jeep flew over a cliff, ejecting us violently. My brother sustained a broken kneecap, and I fractured my pelvis." He attempted to walk for help, but the severe pain stopped him, causing him to collapse in the snow.

Their parents, alarmed, when the boys failed to return home, began a search when daylight appeared. It had snowed about 4 inches overnight and the search party could only guess at the roads the boys had taken. Eventually, they saw what appeared to be a body under the snow. There lay the two boys, still conscious, but severely injured. Both of them lost their legs due to freezing and one lost both hands, their lives spared but not their limbs. In the midst of a tragic situation, this family in crisis felt the ministry of a compassionate Pastor.

In another home a different type of crisis occurred in the lives of a husband and wife who attended Immanuel Church. The husband, a physician, rushed into the room where his wife sat, curling her hair. He weakly, but urgently asked her to take him to a nearby hospital. He cried out, "I'm going under fast! I've taken an entire bottle of sleeping pills." Apparently he was having second thoughts about his foolhardy action.

The medication quickly caused him to lose consciousness prior to arriving at the hospital. Aymond came to pray for him every day, but no movement could be sensed from this comatose patient. On the fourth day, Aymond came into the hospital room and walked to the bed where the man lay positioned on his side. He placed his hand on the patient's thigh and began to pray earnestly, asking God to awaken him from the coma. Suddenly, the patient's body jumped; it seemed several inches, and the fervently praying pastor, startled, did a sudden bounce himself! Thankfully God answered the prayers of many and the man recovered.

Reaching folks for Christ was one of Aymond's priorities in all of his pastorates, no matter the setting. People gave their lives to Christ following the Sunday services, when in the hospital and in their homes. On Sundays, at the conclusion of the invitation, Aymond talked in his office to those who had responded, making certain they understood the message and their decision to follow Christ, which included baptism.

One young man from the island of Cyprus heeded the invitation, and as he and Aymond conversed, Aymond thought it an excellent opportunity to learn from a Greek person the meaning of the word baptizo. In response to Aymond's question he answered, "To cover completely; to put under."

Aymond tells of a debate between a professor at Bethel College and a Lutheran theologian on the subject of baptism. The teacher from Bethel said simply, "Gentlemen, this word baptizo, if properly translated means to immerse," his only argument in the three parts of the debate.

In the years of Aymond's ministry, he baptized many, but none quite as unique as a baptism held in the home of an invalid man in failing health. The man, a Christian, desired earnestly to have Aymond baptize him.

Unable to leave his home caused a brief dilemma regarding the problem of the church baptistry. Being a man of small stature simplified the dilemma. Rising to the occasion, Aymond thought why not the bathtub? So with the man's wife and others present, he testified to his faith in Christ and Aymond immersed him in the family tub.

After three effective years of ministry, the God who brought Aymond and Mildred to the mountain city of Denver, created a

U turn in their lives. Once again responding to the Lord's call, Chicago became home for them a second time. Aymond broadened his role as pastor and became the executive minister of the Midwest Conference. They left the parsonage life style, exchanging it for a unique ministry where Aymond's leadership gifts manifested themselves in an expanded area.

His responsibilities involved planting new churches, assisting established churches and raising funds for present and future needs. Aymond believed church planting is vital to local church growth and worldwide outreach. He coined a phrase, which described the mission he confronted: "If all the world shall ever know, the home base must ever grow."

Ever the 'country boy' at heart, he marveled that God called him once again to minister in the big city. Aymond's fund raising abilities confirmed God's plan in returning him to Chicago. After five years as executive minister, his gifts in this area created an enormous impact. When he arrived, a conference fund existed called the Frontiers Development Fund. The purpose of this fund was for church planting, but as Aymond explained, "it appeared anemic to me, so I set about to better it," and he did.

Aymond's plan to turn a sickly fund into a healthy and useful one involved several steps. First, he personally visited the many people he knew from his eight years of living in Chicago. He asked them to commit to a three year plan and invited them to give $1000.00, or $500.00 a year for a three year period. (He courageously did not suggest smaller figures due to the time required in receiving and handling.)

Subsequently, he made a presentation to the Midwest Conference annual meeting where pastors and church representatives from the Midwest area gathered. An electrician friend helped him make a large exhibit. Complete with electric lights, it displayed the Midwest Conference relationship to mission fields around the world. The resulting impact confirmed Aymond's coined phrase, "If all the world shall ever know, the home-base must ever grow."

At the conclusion of his 5-year term, the board requested Aymond to continue one more year, but at age 64, he felt God calling him to another type of ministry. Aymond prepared to follow God's ongoing plan for his life. When asked his opinion on the difference between local church ministry and that of the district work, he forthrightly replied, "The action in district work is always 'out there,' while in the pastorate it is always right where you are. Thus, the pastor is more in control."

Chapter 10

Persevering in Ministry

$\mathcal{E}$ven though retirement age loomed on the horizon, at age 64, Aymond's pastor's heart couldn't allow him to place his 'shingle' in a drawer, nor hunger for financial security.

Bethel Baptist Church, in Ellison Bay, Wisconsin found itself in a quandary. The winter attendance held at 30–40 people with the financial income unable to compete with the present one. The congregation speculated about disbanding and uniting with the Sister Bay Church. But following concerted prayer, they trusted God's direction and resolved to remain where He had planted them. The future revealed the latter decision as the Lord's.

First on the church's priority list was to seek the man the Lord wanted as their shepherd. Once again asking God for guidance they asked Aymond to consider pastoring Bethel Church. He accepted the challenge in spite of an annual salary of $6000.00. Some parishioners doubted he needed this amount due to having a Social Security income.

As Aymond's preaching became known, more and more people from the community came to the services. Under his effective ministry the attendance occasionally reached 300.

Due to the increase in attendance, the ushers' role grew from passing out bulletins and 'taking up the offering.' They soon

found themselves hurriedly placing additional chairs in the basement and connecting loud speakers so the overflow crowd could
hear, while gratefully thanking God for the growth that was occurring.

Unselfish with 'his' pulpit, Aymond loved to share it with
those who had unusual experiences. These speakers made a definite impact on the congregation. Among them were John Irvin,
chaplain at Cook County jail who spoke on the "The Story of a
Boy, ' and Eunice Kronholm, a bankers wife in St. Paul, Minnesota who told her story of being kidnapped and held for ran-
som.

As pastor at Bethel Church, Aymond once again preached
the Biblical mandate of tithing. 'Hollering' at people about money
was not part of these messages, but he firmly stated his belief
saying, "The story of money is 'so-o-o' fascinating; it is, and I've
got stories to prove it!"

Aymond's gift of raising money harmonized with his compassion for others. Each year Bethel Church set aside a Sunday
to remember the hungry of the world. Aymond prepared the
congregation well in advance of this day. One Sunday, he brought
a message on famine as a sign of the end times. As he preached
and challenged the people about their responsibility, the thought
occurred to him 'why not offer them an opportunity to give now,
this morning?'

An on the spot decision, not discussed with the church board,
Aymond proceeded to ask the congregation for an additional
offering. Touched by the need of the hungry in the world, the
people reached into their pockets, knowing the Lord had directed. The spur of the moment offering resulted in over $900.00
for the world's hungry. Following the service, one woman told
Aymond, "Pastor I emptied the entire content of my purse, $45.72
into the offering plate." Aymond's daughter-in-law capped it all
when she said to him, 'Well, this morning you blew it!" Aymond
wondered how so, thinking, "Did I offend her? Didn't she agree
with me?" With sincerity she replied, "I had $60.00 in a sepa-
rate compartment of my billfold, which I had saved to buy new
skis, and I gave it all!"

On the basis of that Sunday's offering, Aymond suggested a future goal of $1000.00 on the following "Remember the Hungry Day." The next year, this unpretentious church with a membership of 75, gave to the Lord a special offering totaling over $3000.00!

Aymond's conviction on tithing, continued into his extended retirement years. At age 90 Aymond, the guest speaker in the morning service at Bethel Church, preached on that subject. He proclaimed "Nothing is more misunderstood than money and nothing enslaves like money." Continuing he leaned forward, looked into the eyes of the congregation with confident conviction saying, "Now wait a minute! Listen!" As both hands flared out, he claimed, "money can be an extension of our selves. If earned, it represents energy and self. It's like electricity where the switch controls all, and is power. How we release the power will have eternal significance." He later commented, "I would say Bethel is the best giving church around!"

A friend and colleague, Delmar Dahl, recalls Aymond preaching a message on tithing each July when he pastored the Sister Bay Church. Delmar questioned Aymond about this repetition and the reply he received left no doubt as to Aymond's motivation. "I know the message is a good one. They've got money and need to give it to the Lord," he said with firmness. Then with forthrightness he added, "Don't be ashamed of it."

Aymond's strong belief in giving the Lord His due began during one summer he served as student pastor in Wentworth, Wisconsin before returning to Bethel College in the fall. The following summer the Wentworth church invited him to return for a week long series of meetings. An added note on the invitation, requested him 'to be certain to speak on the subject of money.' "Did I ever have to study!" exclaimed Aymond. "Eight sermons on money."

Study he did! He prepared 3 x 5 cards to give to the people the last evening of the series. He had printed, "I will begin giving a tithe of my money beginning next Sunday." Families took the cards home and discussed their responsibility in private. Commitments were made and continued in earnest. This resulted in a dramatic increase in giving to the Lord's work, and also the church's first bank account!

Prior to these messages, the congregation placed their slim offerings in a simple box from which the treasurer withdrew money to pay the bills. When the people began to tithe of their money to the Lord, the church soon built a parsonage and called a full-time pastor. Eventually an educational unit was built and finally a new sanctuary. Aymond considered this as evidence of the Lord's blessing on Christians who understand the true role of money!

Throughout the years of Aymond's ministry he continued to teach his congregations about tithing. Near the end of his full-time ministry, he tells an example of his frugality. "When I came to Ellison Bay, the church budget was a total of $9000.00. So I went to surplus sales and bought some damaged items, some out of my own pocket. Rugs for the Sunday School rooms and behind the pulpit; carpets for additional rooms and high chairs for the nursery; all purchased inexpensively. People appreciated it and had a lot of fun with me," he grinned. "One merchant in the area called me the Rabbi of Gills Rock."

Purchasing items from his own meager income causes one to wonder how he had enough money leftover for his family needs. Aymond justified his deeds by insisting, "Listen! I looked for bargains. I got to know the guy who worked where they made high chairs, so I got five."

"Seriously, I've never robbed God. We've always given more than our tithe. I still believe that old, old well-worn passage of Malachi 3:10 (NIV): 'Bring the whole tithe into the storehouse, that there may be food in my house. Test me in this, says the Lord Almighty, and see if I will not throw open the floodgates of heaven and pour out so much blessing that you will not have room enough for it.' Aymond added, "When I quote this scripture, I stress the blessing might not necessarily be money, but possibly good health."

Mildred confirms her husband's intent. "He showed his love for God as he faithfully tithed. One month, running low on money due to extra bills, he wondered if he could pay half his tithe in the middle of the month instead of in the beginning; his usual plan. Thinking about this, he decided it would be wrong and lacking faith, so he gave his full tithe, leaving us with only $5.00 to live on. He preached faithfulness in tithing to others— how could he do less?"

She continued, "On Tuesday when Aymond came into his office, a man waited for him, requesting money. Aymond gave the visitor $2.00, leaving him with $3.00. The next day the funeral director called, asking Aymond to officiate at a service for which he received $25.00 That same week he received another $25.00 in the mail. Aymond had conducted a funeral and the family sent him compensation. On Friday, he performed an unexpected wedding for which he received $20.00."

Aymond began to wonder if the Lord planned to return the same amount of tithe that he had given when so short of money. On the following Sunday morning, Aymond mischievously said to the Lord, "You're $5.00 short!" The `shortage' no longer existed when a friend reimbursed Aymond for $5.00 he had previously borrowed. As Aymond faithfully tithed, God manifested His faithfulness.

A testimony to his views occurred at a Baptist General Conference meeting in Green Bay, Wisconsin. Aymond wrote a check for $50.00 intending to place it in the offering on Foreign Missions night. During the meeting, the leader declared they would like to receive an offering of $7500.00. At that point, Aymond remembered he had left his check lying on the dresser. At the conclusion of the meeting, it was announced the offering totaled $7450.00—exactly $50.00 short of the goal. Impressed that his $50.00 would have made it, he said, "To me it was not just a coincidence. It showed me how vital is each gift of money."

In addition to preaching the truth God lay on his heart, Aymond's involvement in ministry extended with heart-felt compassion to the neighboring community. The customary warm welcome he received when visiting in the homes occasionally deviated to the frosty. One day he called upon a family where the wife and two sons practiced a different faith from the husband who was 'more or less' involved in the church. The chill that met him at the door surpassed the welcome. It took a tragic event to change this climate.

While at a wedding reception, a phone call came telling Aymond that one of the sons from this family had drowned. He immediately went to the home where the mother sat in deep grief. Aymond learned her son had been her mainstay and he claimed, "I've never seen anyone grieve so hard."

He continued visiting this grieving mom, often bringing Mildred's scrumptious rice pudding and a bowl of fresh raspberries. The mother's trust in Aymond slowly increased. The frostiness began to thaw into a warm and gracious welcome. Much later on a cold, winter day, her husband died. His death occurred during a time Aymond and Mildred had traveled south for the winter.

Aymond later learned, she had said to her son, "Now where is my friend Aymond?" Remembering this time caused a tug at Aymond's heart and tears in his eyes.

Pastor Aymond tried to meet the needs of those from the neighboring community, while not neglecting his own congregation. A woman from Bethel Church, concerned about her husband's spiritual life, asked Aymond to visit him. He went to the man's workshop and chatted with him, while he continued to go about his work. After many such visits, he sensed he had gained the confidence of this very shy man and began to broach the subject of spiritual matters.

Aymond always made it a policy to be alone with the one he spoke to about their spiritual life, not wanting them to feel outnumbered. Ultimately, Aymond sensed the time was right and as they talked in the man's workshop, Aymond confronted him directly about his need for Christ. The heart of this non-believer, primed by the Holy Spirit, joined the ranks of believers that day acknowledging Christ as his Savior. At the mid-week service he told the people, "I never dreamed I would receive Christ as my Savior while in my workshop dressed in overalls."

He told Aymond, "I'm no good as a speaker, but I will do what I can." Faithful to his promise, he cheerfully served the Lord by using his house painting skills whenever needed.

Aymond quoted from Colossians 3:14, "Over all these virtues put on love, which binds them all together in perfect unity." To Aymond this new Christian "was in full-time service as much as the one who stands behind the pulpit. So-o-o great!"

Ever ready to lead others to Christ, Aymond learned he needed to clear up misconceptions first. While visiting another man in his home, Aymond challenged him about the importance of becoming a Christian. The man's perception of the church and salvation proved inaccurate when he answered, "But this is not a church." It seemed impossible such an important step could be taken apart from a church building. Following Aymond's explanation of the scripture, he too chose a new life in Christ.

Mildred and Aymond consider the ministry at Bethel Church inspirationally comparable to any of their pastorates. After eleven fruitful years of pastoring full-time at Bethel Church, 75 year old Aymond concluded the time had come to 'sort' of retire.

'Sort of' meant part-time ministry. Thus he and Mildred left their cozy parsonage and the people they loved, moving a short distance south to Sturgeon Bay. Here he began as interim pastor at the First Baptist Church. Aymond felt a deep concern for this daughter church of Ellison Bay; another group experiencing financial difficulties.

The slim budget of the church could not tolerate a badly needed upgrading for the parsonage. Aymond realized the urgent financial needs of this church had to become one of his immediate priorities.

Employing his gift of raising money, Aymond devised an ingenious plan. He approached seven friends from his former pastorate at Ellison Bay, and asked them each to make a loan for a period of four years. The terms would be $1000.00 for three years at 10% interest. It sounded good, but a major problem existed. The church didn't have funds to pay the 10% interest! Aymond would not think of asking anything for himself, but this was the Lord's work, so he surged on. With boldness, he asked these men if they would be willing to return the interest as a gift, which they readily agreed to. Through their generosity,

$7000.00 was raised, and the men of the First Baptist Church donated a large chunk of time and effort resulting in a beautiful parsonage.

Following six months of interim ministry in Sturgeon Bay, Aymond and Mildred joined the snowbirds, and moved to sunny Florida, leaving the blast of Wisconsin winters behind. Arriving in Florida, his ministry 'shingle' failed to hide in a drawer to exchange for the sunny beaches of Florida. At age 76, he joined the staff of Bethel Baptist Church in Bradenton, Florida where he ministered part-time for the next four years.

Intense study and teaching continued to keep his days and evenings full, as he led the mid-week service and taught the adult Sunday School. He loved his 'super' Sunday morning class. He used "God's Solutions to Man's Problems," as the basis for his teaching, embellishing it with his own resources. Both teaching sessions overflowed in attendance during the winter months, due to Aymond's matchless teaching skills and the influx of 'snow-birds' from the north.

When the snow and ice disappeared in Wisconsin, Aymond and Mildred left the torrid heat of Florida. They returned to beautiful Door County anticipating life on their lovely farm for the summer and fall months. Ministry for Aymond didn't end during these months as he continued to preach as supply pastor and teach Sunday school classes into his 90 + years. The weekday work around the farm sometimes waited while he persevered in ministry, visiting those who didn't know his Lord, the ill and people needing his touch of compassion.

Chapter 11

Prayers, Vegies and Collectibles

*A*ymond's intended life of planting seeds and harvesting crops evolved into sowing God's word in the soil of human hearts, and sharing in the harvest of people for the Lord. Following an abundant pastoral ministry, the Lord returned to Aymond what he had relinquished many years ago. In 1974, while pastoring in Ellison Bay, Wisconsin, Aymond, and Mildred purchased a lovely farm along Highway 42 close to the tip of the Door County thumb.

Visitors to the Anderson's "Friendly Acres" farm know a warm welcome awaits them. Driving on the busy highway where vehicles transport the many tourists and the deliverymen hurriedly racing by, they welcome the sight of the peaceful farm setting. Towering Cottonwood and Popple trees present an archway for the visitor to drive under as they enter the yard. Immediately ahead stands a two story, one car, white garage surrounded on either side by masses of gorgeous Cosmos, Roses, Canterbury Bells and a climbing purple Clematis, all planted and cared for by Mildred. Mature Lilac bushes define the yard north of their home.

A short distance to the right of the garage stand two small, white structures. Mildred claims the first as her sewing house where her capable hands produce intricate designs on clothing she has created, and lovely household items. A few steps farther, the best 'john' in Door County is located, according to Aymond. Complete with contoured seats and pictures on the wall, he claims it is impossible to tip over. A friend claims, "The 'john' is so clean, I wouldn't use it!"

To the right of the driveway is the home Mildred and Aymond love. The delightful old, chink log structure built in 1881 increased in size with the eventual construction of additional rooms. A small white porch leading into the back hall and kitchen is used as a main entry. A larger porch across the front of the home offers an enchanting invitation to relax in white rockers and enjoy the beauty of red geraniums hanging from the porch roof.

As visitors walk toward the kitchen entrance, they pass a swing hanging motionless from a tall tree, peacefully awaiting grandchildren to give it action. Aymond opens the door and greets his visitors with a sly grin and a hurried "Come in, come in," causing one to wonder what he has up his sleeve!

Evidence of his love for antiques fill the walls and shelf of the small hallway. Various lanterns, some left from the days of railroad work, cow bells, numerous keys, 'strap on' ice skates, a coffee grinder and butter maker remind the viewer of days past. Even two age-old toasters and a telephone with a crank needed to reach the operator, are only a minuscule of his collection from years gone by.

With a welcoming smile and a warm, "I'm so glad to have you in our home," Mildred greets her guests in her blue and white kitchen next to the hallway. Adjacent, is the dining room, which functions akin to a family room. A round oak table claims center stage, graced with flowers from Mildred's garden. When invited for a cup of coffee following evening church services, lucky guests will be seated around the table and served one of Mildred's luscious pies. This treat often follows a game of Crazy Eight with Aymond emphatically calling out the rules, loudly exclaiming, "No, no—now listen!!"

Sometimes guests are seated in the living room to visit while Mildred finishes preparations in the kitchen. From the dining room, visitors walk past a stairway leading to the upstairs bedrooms.

Precious family wedding pictures grace the stairwell. Aymond proudly points out the appealing picture of his parents. Continuing into the living room, an antique pump organ stands against one wall and Mildred's piano on another. Many of son Dan's exceptional black and white photographs hang in this room and also throughout the home.

While visiting in the living room, Aymond takes delight in displaying a few of his antique treasures. A favorite is a 'cupping set;' a blood letting tool given to him by a woman whose mother was a practitioner. He exposes the 10 bladed knife that made small cuts on the skin explaining, "after the skin was cut, a cup containing a valve, was placed over the opening. Then a syringe was inserted which sucked out the 'bad' blood." Gratefully, this now abandoned practice occurred in the 1800's to 1900's.

When the visitors are ready to leave, they cherish the loving welcome they've felt and the laughter they experienced, departing with a sense of yearning to return.

The half-circle driveway leading back to the highway takes guests past two more buildings. A white barn located to the right conceals its unbelievable, antique filled interior including an enormous number of farm implements. Another low, white building is poised ready to welcome guests. This former chicken coop, turned book bindery, then evolved into an office for a lumber broker, now is transformed into a charming guest house created by Mildred's impressive decorating and sewing skills.

Antique farm equipment rests on either side of the driveway. A 100-year-old plow and a rusted hay rake stand deserted after countless years of farm work. Nearby, archaic ice tongs rest on a large stone adding further interests for eager antique seekers.

Departing from this enchanting farm, one is reminded of Aymond and Mildred's faithfulness in ministry, but more importantly of their God who assured His children, "To the faithful you show yourself faithful." Psalm 18:25 (NIV)

Retirement for Aymond can best be defined as pressing on for His Lord. Yet this era in his life has also included several embarrassing moments when he landed topside, rather than on his intended feet, taking one of his famous plunges to the terra firma.

One sunny day the 'farmer' Aymond met face to face with a few carrots. Carrying a container of water in each hand, he walked into the garden, ready to prove his agricultural skills. Unseen, a piece of netting lay on the ground with green grass poking through the openings. Suddenly, both of Aymond's feet became entangled in the web and he catapulted to the ground. Dazed, he moved his legs and arms and figured they still worked. As his eyes opened he stared at the healthy carrot tops fanning his face. Not one to ignore even vegetables, he spoke to them saying, "Aren't you glad the Lord has given me strong bones?" After making his way home, Mildred hearing the story, was duly impressed and amazed once again, to think her husband not only survived without injury, but also talked to vegetables!

Instead of carrots observing his catastrophe, two women witnessed another plight, causing him considerable embarrassment. Having purchased two gallons of milk at the grocery store, he walked across the parking lot carrying the bottles in each hand. Without warning, his face, again made contact with the ground. One milk jug exploded, causing him to wonder "what now!" Not aware of tripping on anything, he picked himself up, mystified and mortified, and headed for the refuge of his truck. The women observing this scenario, checked to make certain he was all right, informing him he had a loop of plastic on his ankle.

Bleeding from his cut lip and elbow, he decided it best to explain his predicament to the store manager. In doing so, he learned a plastic loop used to bind bundles of grocery bags together, had not been cut, and somehow landed in the checkout lane. As Aymond walked to the car, it had unknowingly become tangled around his foot. Satisfied, his next stop was to the local doctor, who patched him up.

Aymond knew others might consider this episode an open and shut lawsuit. The insurance company, apprehensive about the same possibility, showed their concern with letters and phone calls. However, Aymond's value system would not allow him to sue a friend.

When not speaking to carrots or tangled in plastic, his valuable and fascinating antique collection involves time and absorbs Aymond's free hours.

Collecting and restoring 'old' things has become a wonderful hobby. When wintering in Florida, he combs the flea markets searching for the unique. Auctions and garage sales are frequented, and as a friend claims, 'there isn't an attic in Door County Aymond hasn't been in.' Aymond knows how to take the old and restore it to its original beauty claiming, "I receive great satisfaction from bringing things back to their former condition. While I work with them, I visualize the people that used these treasures." As the barn quickly fills with a myriad of impressive antiques, Mildred questions him asking, "What would I do with them if 'something' happens to you?"

Aymond began to pray about her question. Friends advised him to start a museum and charge a fee; others recommended he open an antique shop. Neither appealed to him, as he coveted his freedom. God knew Aymond's concern, and as a result, he feels one of the greatest answers to his prayers had commenced year's prior.

While pastoring at Bethel Church in Ellison Bay, children from a nearby summer camp, attended the Sunday church services. Jeff Weborg from Bethel Church had become a good friend with the camp director, Dean Matson. When Dean moved to California, Jeff visited him and there he met a young man with a hobby of collecting 'old things.' Jeff remarked he knew a 'weirdo' (Aymonds' quote) in Ellison Bay who had a nice antique collection. The man eventually traveled to Wisconsin, and when he saw Aymond's antiques, purchased the entire collection. Friends helped load a large U-Haul filling it with cherished relics. Once again, Aymond heeded, with wonder, the power of prayer!

Did this relieve Mildred's anxiety about what to do with all the 'stuff'? Perhaps for a brief time, but before long the barn once again filled with Aymond's treasures. Spending winters in Florida proved a 'gre-a-a-t' time to search for treasures, but he needed to find a way to transport them to Wisconsin. Friends driving to Wisconsin heard his plea of "You got room in your car for two packages? Just two, just two!"

Mildred feels this is a wonderful hobby for Aymond and claims, "It gives me so much pleasure to see the enjoyment he derives from his collecting; just as he enjoys the privilege of serving the Lord when speaking and ministering to others."

Called upon to demonstrate his antiques at a Sunday School teachers' dinner held at Bethel Church, at Seaquist Orchards, or in front of his barn for touring visitors, his viewers are all fascinated as they view and listen to Aymond's tales of relics from the past. Residents of the Meadows in Sister Bay, the Kiwanis, and a tour from the Twin Cities, are among those who came by bus to view memories from their grandparents and parents' day, as well as a few unexpected treasures.

He not only loves to display and explain his antiques, but he equally enjoys the fun of teasing others with his 'treasures.' On one occasion visitors driving into Aymond's yard heard a loud siren screaming from the confines of his garage. Hearing the car, Aymond had cranked the handle on his 'plaything' emitting a shrill sound designed to startle the weak. His 'toy' turned out to be an antique fire engine siren from the days when electronic push buttons didn't exist.

With a sense of delight, Aymond takes his friends into the very orderly and clean barn where round sleigh bells from Austria, skates and antique pitchforks hang. Lying on tables covered with protective cloths are a myriad of antique tools each painstakingly soaked in a solution of water, and "any amount of Lye, on the condition it is good metal. If wood, of course you've gotta be careful." He continued, "also any amount of ammonia. As the tools soak for days, weeks, whatever, they're saturated with the solution, and then I follow by polishing them to their original beauty. That's it!"

Walking through the barn, one feels as though the 20th century has yet to happen as it is filled with artifacts from the 18th and 19th centuries. Proudly, Aymond lifts more cloths off the antiques, exposing unusually beautiful discoveries. Cow bells, an iron from China, an ancient ice cream maker, and scoop, all lying in an organized fashion. When he uncovers still more cloths, a fish scaler and four-sided toaster lay exposed. The assortment also includes a cap gun, which he playfully shoots with a 'crack, crack,' (he's fond of the smell and sound), a school bell and a left-handed 1911 vacuum. Nearby an American flag is hung, proudly displaying 45 stars. Continuing through the barn, he picks up a pop bottle containing a marble that emits a POP. "Doesn't that do something?" he grins. Mildred smiles and remarks simply, "It doesn't.

Reluctantly leaving the tools of yesteryear behind, yet with a happy anticipation of what awaits at the top of the steps, Aymond takes his visitors to his second floor 'one of a kind' office. Entering the garage through a side door one must climb very steep steps. Arriving slightly breathless, his friends are grateful they made the climb.

On the walls additional pictures from bygone days hang. Aymond points out one of the most meaningful pictures to him, which is one of David and Dennis, his sons in their younger years.

His crowded and cluttered office is filled with books, papers, personal memorabilia, and not unanticipated, more antiques! He offers a seat in his worn office chair, while he proudly points out an antique meat grinder. A helmet from France containing a bullet hole hangs on the wall, as do hornets nests and additional sleigh and cowbells. A prized wooden cash register, various hand held fans, lovely old jewelry, and a fly swatter screen are scattered throughout the room.

Innumerable books line the walls and are stacked on his desk. A valuable accumulation of letters from the past conceals the old wooden desktop. More significant to him than all the possessions from the past are individual pictures of his four boys and Mildred, hanging on the wall next to his desk. Trying to conceal a proud father's smile, he uncovers a folder and produces a perfectly drawn picture of football players in action drawn by his son Dennis. "Perrfect!" he exclaims. "Aren't they just grreat!" I agreed!

When the tour is completed, it becomes necessary to gingerly descend the steps from his office. Clutching the railing and careful of each step, the invited feel they have experienced an extraordinary privilege to witness his memory filled office. More importantly, this room, in the midst of disarray, is a revered place of prayer.

Here Aymond keeps his disciplined appointment with God. Early each morning he climbs the steps to this sanctuary above the garage. It is in this room his day begins as he talks to the Lord. "Gets kind of loud sometimes," he grinned. "These times have been a real joy to me and I look forward to them."

Aymond says, "One thing I have come to be so grateful for in 'retirement,' is time for prayer which is so meaningful to me. During ministry I was so 'cotton-pickin' busy—must do, must do. Always rush, rush and so many demands; many times (not always) prayer did not have the priority it should have." Aymond's mother was a great woman of prayer and he states, "that's how she hung in there."

During difficult situations in Aymond's ministry he wrote and dated his prayer requests in a notebook and prayerfully placed them in the Lord's trusted hands. One simple request read, "Lord, here is a situation I just can't handle and I ask You to take over."

A lesson about patience in prayer occurred when Aymond searched for a friend from Moody with whom he had lost contact. The two men had developed a close friendship, enjoying time together. On one occasion they attended the Billy Graham crusade in New York City together.

Eventually Aymond learned the friend "kind of wandered off the straight and narrow, and moved into the commune system." Aymond began to pray about the situation, earnestly wanting to locate him. He checked telephone directories of cities as he traveled. One day a flash of inspiration happened. Knowing the friend had attended Moody, he thought, "I'll give it a shot." He contacted the school and obtained his address. After twenty years of praying and searching, his prayer was answered. He learned his friend had cast off the commune life style and became pastor of a small church. "It was so grre-at to see him; a grre-at experience," he exclaimed.

An important part of Aymond's prayer time is his use of the Living Bible. As he searched and prayed for his friend, he claimed the scripture from Psalm 42:11. "Don't be discouraged, don't be upset, expect God to act! For I know that I shall again have plenty of reason to praise him for all that he will do . . ." (Living Bible). Knowing God will answer in *His* time, Aymond claims, "We must hang in there when praying."

During his private prayer time Aymond follows a scriptural progression as he begins with its claims.

From Psalm 55:22. "Give your burdens to the Lord, He will carry them. (Living Bible).

Psalm 42:11. (Quoted above).

James 5:16. ". . .The earnest prayer of a righteous man has great power and wonderful results." (Living Bible) To this scripture, Aymond says assuredly, "I can pray just as effectively as Elijah, for in Christ I am just as righteous as He."

Genesis 32:26. Jacob tells the Lord ". . . I will not let you go until you bless me." (Living Bible)

Acts 16:14 tells about Lydia whose heart the Lord opened. In response to this scripture Aymond avows "this has been a great lesson to me. It is not my job to open people's hearts; that I cannot do. It does not matter how rusty or corroded the heart's lock has become. The Holy Spirit is perfectly and totally equipped to do so, having the spiritual WD-40, and the spiritual 'wrenches, pliers and screw drivers.' He has a special key suited for every person in the world." He adds "These thoughts have been a source of great encouragement to me as I pray for many people others might think beyond the reach of the Gospel."

Giving the Lord his basic hopes, he claims Heb. 11:1 (Living Bible) . . "What is faith? It is the confident assurance that something we want is going to happen. It is the certainty that what we hope for is waiting for us, even though we cannot see it up ahead."

Finally, John 14:13 and 14. ". . .You can ask Him for anything, using my name, and I will do it, for this will bring praise to the Father because of what I, the Son, will do for you."

John 16:23, 24: "At that time you won't need to ask me for anything, for you can go directly to the Father and ask Him, and He will give you what you ask for because you use my name. You haven't tried this before, (but begin now). Ask, using my name, and you will receive, and your cup of joy will overflow!" (Living Bible)

Concluding his comments on prayer, Aymond declares, "I came to know something of what that name really involves. Into that name, (that God gave Him) is poured everything imaginable that *could* be used and *must* be used to bring people to Christ or cause a believer to grow."

Confirming his deep prayer life, is the one closest to Aymond, his wife. "I appreciate his personal devotional persistence—he depends on this totally. I have been so inspired by his faith and consistent Christian walk—one based on I COR. 13, the love chapter, from which he preached so much and so convincingly. His spiritual side is such an all-encompassing thing in his life that it isn't really separate. His sleeping habits get him up early. On occasion I have awakened at daybreak and observed him lying on his back, eyes closed, with hands folded and lips moving in prayer.

"On most mornings, he might make a fire in the stove; then make his way to his quiet place—in early years his office—later years his study over the garage. Here he finds a communion and nearness to God that we can never fully enter into. In his study, he has a wall of pictures by his desk of our four boys and me. As he prayed for each one, he would place his hands on the one he prayed for, one by one until all were covered. I took a picture of the wall so he could take it to Florida and keep his visible prayer objects with him.

"His Living Bible shows how the book of Psalms ministered to him in various circumstances. When sticky situations arose, and then became resolved, he would tell me, 'D' you know? I just asked the Lord to handle it and He did."

Chapter 12

Ministry Energized By Love Continues

A young church attender once asked his pastor what he did during the week. "Do you have another job?" he questioned. As he observed him preaching on Sundays, it seemed safe to assume his pastor had either additional employment or enjoyed a soft life between Sundays. To those who possess similar thoughts, Aymond reiterates the schedule he followed and then shares his views on ministry today.

"My instructor at Moody made it clear one must spend considerable time in sermon preparation. He taught us, 'don't ever think you need not study, expecting the Holy Spirit will give you words to speak when you stand before your congregation. If that is what you depend on, He will fill you with hot air.'"

Early Monday morning, Aymond began the groundwork for the following Sunday message while seated at his desk. A unique file system became an invaluable asset to his message preparation and is one he used throughout his ministry. He continues to draw from its yellowed and worn files, even though now the file is located on the first floor of his garage; much too heavy to consider hauling up the narrow steps to his office. He is proud of this priceless system, but much discipline and time is required to keep it updated. An abundance of stimulating resource material has proved its worth not only to him, but this system has contributed invaluable help to other pastors as well.

Aymond differentiates pulling ideas out of a file, in contrast to *the most* resourceful and trustworthy method. "The Lord gives me thoughts which I've never read when I lie awake at night. I immediately write them on the pad of paper kept at my bedside."

Disciplined in preparation and proficient in delivery, he is so thankful for the gift of evangelism the Lord gave to him. Using this gift, he conducted evangelistic meetings twice a year extending for a period of 40 years; all this in addition to his pastorates. Following his messages at home or away, Aymond generally gave his listeners an opportunity to walk to the front of the sanctuary and publicly declare their faith in Jesus Christ. When asked if this method of evangelism works today, he replied, "That's one thing I've asked the Lord; show what You did years ago, so they know You did it."

Whether preaching in his church or conducting out of town meetings, God has used Aymond's distinctly unique method of preaching. A Moody Monthly magazine article, "Do Fundamental Preachers Have To Be Dull?" made a distinct impact on his ministry. "I didn't read books on sermon preparation, because they don't talk like me! I'm not a manuscript preacher. Those things make me so nervous. Rather than preaching verse by verse, I take subjects starting where the people are, apply the Bible and just talk."

Aymond remembers a special Sunday when he preached at the Bethel Church on Washington Island. Unknown to him at the time, a journalist, editor, and winner of seven literary awards sat in the congregation. Mr. Elwell Crissey had also authored a remarkable book, "Lincoln's Lost Speech."

The following Sunday Mr. Crissey attended services at Bethel Baptist in Ellison Bay where Aymond pastored. He spoke with Aymond following the service and the next week Aymond received a letter from him. In it he told of hearing many great speakers and felt Aymond's pulpit competence ranked him right along side of them. He then requested copies of Aymond's sermon series on love and sent him his 424-page book on Lincoln.

Pastor Delmar Dahl describes Aymond as an "exciting preacher, one who held firmly to his beliefs. If he felt incapable of doing something, he could say no without fear. No doubt, whether it be as full-time pastor or as an interim, he brought a positive attitude with excitement and plenty of pizzazz."

In spite of his effectiveness as a preacher and pastor, Aymond would make priority changes in his ministry if he could begin anew. "I would continue to put study at the top of my list. Yet, in retrospect, I'd devote more time to prayer in all areas of my life, as I've come to know it now, i.e. the ministry and my sons. I think prayer is number one in thinking of change." He firmly believes the Bible is a basic resource book, but at times it becomes (to some), merely another religious book. "If I were a pastor again, I would have the congregation read the Ten Commandments every Sunday."

His compassion for the younger generation is evident in his preaching. One Sunday while preaching to an overflow congregation in the Ellison Bay Church, he stopped and eyeballed the young people seated in front of him. Raising both hands and waving his flat thumb, he said explicitly, "Now listen, this is a biggie! An awful biggie! You have personal value. Know God loves you! If God is for you, no one can be against you! This is a foundation to live by. It is impossible to live without God!"

Continuing his message, he told of a girl, Karen Cheng from California, who obtained a perfect score on her SAT test. A brilliant, yet typical teenager, she was asked, "In your opinion, what is the meaning of life?" She answered, "I haven't the faintest idea." Aymond's declaration, Know God loves you! cannot exclude the many teenage suicides. The seemingly avalanche of self-destruction weighed heavily on his heart as he spoke to a group of adults. He challenged them to show love and interest in the younger generation. "Now hear this!" he ordained. "Here's a biggie! An awful biggie! This is very important—very important! We are born with a desire for human companionship. To be shut out is very hard. A supreme lesson of life is to learn what tomorrow says about our actions of today."

During the seventy plus years of Aymond's ministry he has witnessed innumerable transformations occurring in the life of the church. The most significant change he observes, has been the availability of knowledge. "The 'pew' is more knowledgeable, uninhibited and free to express opinions, resulting in higher expectations. Pastors have numerous resources available, i.e., libraries, videos, computers, seminars, and an avalanche of books.

"If I were in the pastorate today, I would speak loud and clear saying that all Christians are in full-time service; all have gifts of one kind or another, and each is equally useful if dedicated to God. Whoever coined phrases like 'the clergy and the laity,' 'the pulpit and the pew,' were not inspired by God. In spite of the vast resources, I feel it is harder to be a pastor today. Formerly, people placed us on a pedestal, but we also coped with 'toughies' in our ministry.

"Secondly, the idea of ministry has changed. A shepherd of souls includes ministering outside the congregation. Servanthood has faded; ministry parallels a profession equated with business. *Instead*, it must be a higher calling."

Asked to comment on other changes he has experienced over the years, i.e. church growth methods, elimination of the Sunday evening service and variation in styles of worship, he replied with conviction, "We must come face to face with people. Telemarketing is legitimate, but the telephone can't be the end. Churches pattern after the mega church, but many components must fit, or it won't work."

He continues, "The Willow Creek Church in Illinois has a logo; 'You matter to God.' Every church should pattern after this *basic* element. A successful businessman and friend attended Willow Creek. When he heard the message 'you matter to God,' he felt hit between the eyes! We can't fulfill ministry, by simply singing choruses and forget the basics that existed yesterday and continue today.

Ministry Energized By Love Continues

"As for the evening service, nowhere does the Bible instruct in the frequency of worship services. Some refuse to 'let go.' When we encourage people to attend these services, we are obligated to entertain them. If it doesn't fit and becomes a drag, forget it," Aymond asserts.

"The old hymns are meaningful and written out of a deep need. They express the writer's spiritual battles and recognize the help, assurance and comfort that alone has its source in the Lord. That is why they seem to effectively minister to people today as well as those of yesterday. Several of my favorites are "I Have Decided to Follow Jesus," "Amazing Grace," "Jesus Lover Of My Soul" and "Rock Of Ages."

"The worship songs of today are simple and fit in. Sometimes it is hard for me to appreciate modern Christian music. Yet, if this music can effectively draw people to Christ, it surely has a place in ministry."

Occasionally pastors encounter frustration when their ministry is not progressing according to well-laid plans. Yet, Aymond denies experiencing this. "Various people bothered me somewhat," he grinned, but added, "I didn't lose sleep over it. There are pastors who feel they're not doing their job, if they aren't in control. We need to be charitable and remember people aren't robots."

His keen sense of humor, coupled with a zest for living and a confident demeanor can easily mislead others. Speaking openly he honestly admits, "I still struggle, feeling inferior and self-conscious, especially when pastors get together—trying to 'one-up each other.' It has helped that I've been asked to speak at many Baptist General Conference meetings, but that still doesn't inflate my ego."

He added, "When I think of the fact that God loves me and accepts me as I am, it makes a difference, but it's easy to forget. It doesn't snow me under, however. I feel in command when I preach and know my subject, but I've never preached a sermon that totally satisfied me. I've been asked if I ever doubted the Truth that I preach. Some days I don't feel one bit saved, but we can't go by feelings. I return to the Word, reminding myself of what it promises: 'All that the Father gives me will come to me and whoever comes to me I will never drive away.' John 6:37"

The 'must do' years of full-time ministry transitioning to the 'do if I want to' retirement years, did not evolve into a drastic change. "Retirement came gradually as I immediately began an interim pastorate, barely caught my breath and became a part-time staff member in a Florida church. I spent a great deal of time writing and studying for lessons I taught.

"Presently, I have opportunities for visitation, preaching and teaching. People who are ill or hurting from various life experiences welcome a visit, along with a bag of apples, some fresh fish, or Mildred's rice pudding. I left farming behind so as to prepare for the ministry, and now the Lord has given me back a farm," he reiterates. Aymond doesn't recount the many phone calls he continues to make across the country to those in need, ill, or wrestling with personal problems.

When asked what advice he would offer young people facing the years ahead of pastoring, he gives an authentic and time-tested method. "There's a simple formula to follow:

- First, genuinely love people.
- Second, work hard (including prayer, study, and visitation).
- Third, use common sense.

"Realize the ministry is different from other occupations. One needs to feel 'called' of God; i.e. unless you're certain of a divine calling you'll never be fully satisfied in the ministry. A forty-hour week and high salaries will not be a priority. There is no greater sense of satisfaction than to be a source of help, comfort and counsel to people in their pilgrimage through life as they head to that city 'whose builder and maker is God.' During the first years of ministry I felt judgmental, but the Holy Spirit generated a change within."

One word sums up Aymond's ministry: LOVE!

Chapter 13

Ironing, Antics and Rice Pudding

The congregation of Bethel Baptist Church listened quietly as the pianist and organist played together in beautiful harmony. Seated in the back row, in *his* special 'spot' next to the aisle, Aymond listened with special interest while Mildred played the piano in perfect accord with the organist LaVerne Madvig. To those seated near him, Aymond exclaimed with a resounding 'whisper,' "I can't believe she's in her 80's!" (Neither could anyone else).

At a later date he voiced additional sentiments: "She's always been a beautiful woman. I look at her playing the piano or organ in church and I think boy she's pretty. I tell her too."

Aymond and Mildred have shown a deep respect for one another. He loves to tease her and both have enjoyed a tremendous amount of fun together. Each has allowed the other to develop their God given gifts. Throughout their years of marriage they have served as role models to the many their lives have touched.

Aymond's partner in life and his greatest asset shares her view of their lives together. She sums it up simply as, "Life with Aymond has been a hoot!"

Prior to Bethel College and meeting Aymond, Mildred had certain grandiose ideas for her future. These ideas centered on using her gifts of music. Mildred's dad wanted her to play a harp, but a teacher was not available. Eventually, she obtained a Vibra harp, receiving her first lesson from Clair Musser who produced these instruments and also taught percussion at Northwestern University. Thus, began a lifetime ministry enriching others with her musical talents on the vibra harp and the piano.

She eventually became a student at Bethel College. One day she attempted to study in the library, when a seminary student sitting across from her blurted out, "D'ya know—you'd make a good pastor's wife." Not knowing what he had in mind, she retorted, "Well, that's the last thing I want to be!" With that proclamation the subject ended, whatever his intentions.

In spite of the sincere plans she had concerning her future, God spoke to Mildred through His Word, resulting in her commitment to follow wherever He might lead. Lead He has, and after 60 years of marriage she could honestly say, "Being a pastor's wife is one of the greatest privileges I could have."

Throughout their pastorates, Aymond made certain Mildred's musical abilities were manifested; even when she feared it could be overdone. At times, when the church had sufficient musicians she enjoyed a rare opportunity to simply listen, 'filling in' when needed. On many evenings bedtime didn't come for her till the wee hours, as she stayed awake to arrange vocal and instrumental music in the correct key. To Mildred this was 'a labor of love.'

Mildred attempts to hide the pride she feels when she speaks of their four sons. Yet, as one sees the glow on her face, it is easy to understand her delight in each of them. Dan the first born, is a retired Endodontist and a black and white photo artist recognized nationwide (according to a newspaper article announcing one of his shows); Dick an electrical contractor, born 23 months after Dan, is the funny bone of the family and Dan's best friend. After 5 more years, Dave and Dennis completed the family 21 months apart. They are both in the same electrical business and are best friends. "We are so grateful for four lovely daughters in-law. Dawn (Dan), Jeannie (Dick), Sue (Dave), Josie (Dennis). "Admittedly with every pregnancy, I wanted a girl, but I wouldn't trade any of my boys. We are so blessed! We have 10 grandchildren (including a set of twins) and nine great-grandchildren."

Echoes from the years of raising children continue to resound in a mom's ears. Mildred happily shares a few delightful tales:

Dennis, a 'sweet little fun' boy often played with Ruthie from next door. Mildred retains a clear picture of the two children sitting together in a mink cage, belonging to Ruthie's Grandpa. One day Aymond served as baby-sitter when both mom's were not at home. Apparently he became distracted and missed a hair-cutting session as Dennis gave Ruthie a most unflattering and abbreviated haircut, causing her mom a lengthy period of un-happiness while waiting for longer hair to appear.

A major heart-stopping event occurred when David and Dennis played 'microphone' with an old vacuum cleaner cord. One end stayed plugged into a wall plate and the other became the imagined mike. Unfortunately a corner of Bakelite had broken off, exposing a portion of metal. When David, the performer held the mike near his mouth, it stuck to his tongue and like lightening; an electric current seared across it penetrating into his tongue two-thirds deep. He remembers only seeing a bright yellow light.

Yet, how could David be walking on this earth today? His older brother sat reading in a chair only three feet away, had no part in it, oblivious to the crisis occurring nearby. Instead, Dennis, the hero, pulled the plug simply for the angry reason that it was his turn with the mike, and he intended to have it!

Parents came to the rescue and took David to Children's Hospital. Here they were told the 'comforting' news that they had never seen such a case and then sent the family home with instructions to observe for swelling so as to prevent him from choking. In the middle of the night the watchful parents checked him and saw a tongue resembling a red ball protruding from his mouth. David did recover, but a scar remains as a reminder of the hazards of performing what could have been his only performance!

One sad day the family sat around the kitchen table sharing Dan's grief. His beloved dog Sandy had been hit by a car and killed. As they talked about their feelings for the pet, Dick's blue eyes suddenly widened and he questioned, "Are we gonna eat him?" Supposedly, he reasoned that when chickens are dead, we eat them, so why not a dog?

Dick and Dan resembled each other as children, but Dick with the longer lashes let people know 'he had more fur around his eyes.'

Prior to Dan and Dawn's marriage, Dawn spent the night at Mildred and Aymond's vacation cottage. Excitement reigned at the prospect of a daughter in the family. After Dawn had gone to bed, Mildred, 'the wanna-be' mother of a daughter, took Dawn's tennis shoes and scrubbed them 'til snow white, not realizing dirty tennis shoes were 'in' at the time. In the morning Dawn saw her gleaming shoes, and thought, "Oh no, I'll just have to get them dirty again!"

Looking back on the children's younger years, Mildred also shares the time Dan went through 5 major operations, braces, and casts due to severely clubbed feet. "We did lots of traveling to medical centers. One day Dan sat on his Daddy's lap in a hospital waiting room. Observing other children sitting in wheel chairs and some lying on carts, he said "Daddy I'm so glad you had my feet fixed!"

The time came when Dan at 8 years of age no longer needed his walking casts which were necessary to straighten his feet. His Sunday School class would be running a race and he wanted to participate. Mildred tried to discourage him thinking he'd come in at the tail end, but knew of his need to be like his friends. In spite of a mom's concerns, he ran the race and came in first place! His heavy casts had strengthened his muscles as he walked and the handicap no longer existed. Mildred said, "I cheered for him and cried for joy." She gratefully added, "His feet have carried him through years of dentistry, skating, skiing the western slopes, and on many a golf course."

A joyful time for any mom is leading a child to Christ. One evening the Christian radio station broadcast a true story on "Unshackled." Mildred noticed David listening with unusual attentiveness. At bath time, he said to his mother, "I want Jesus to forgive my sins too." Mildred said, "It was such a thrill for me to kneel by the bathtub that night and lead my little boy to Jesus."

Mildred loved her two roles of being mom to her boys and a pastor's wife. She viewed them both as a privilege, but admits the second role often scared her. "I remember feeling almost overwhelmed at times, especially when the children were young and Aymond was out of town on speaking engagements."

At times she longed to work outside her home (and later receive a pension). Yet, she questions where she could have found time to work. Each week she ironed 22 starched and sprinkled (no perma press) white shirts for the five men in their household, plus everyday school clothes. Two of the boys had after school jobs requiring clean white shirts daily, including Sundays. In those days, pastors didn't wear sport shirts to the office or when visiting people in their home or hospital.

Besides ironing all those shirts, when did Mildred have time to make her delicious rice puddings when Aymond requested it? He loved to give them to the shut-ins and bereaved when visiting them in their homes. Mildred remembers one week especially. Aymond had requested her rice pudding service several times, and on this particular day, he told her he needed another by 1 P.M. Mildred confessed, "I balked. I told Aymond I just can't get anything else done." Whereupon he replied, "All right I'll do it." He asked Mildred for the recipe and made the pudding. According to Mildred "It turned out good and I felt smitten!" Aymond claims "Mildred's rice pudding has led many to the Lord." The story she claims as her favorite is from the daughter of a rice pudding recipient. "When mom died, the last thing in her stomach was rice pudding." She apparently died happy!

The brimful life of a ministry family disallows maximum time together; therefore when they have the opportunity to enjoy one another, it is precious. Mildred delights in telling about Aymond's antics. "I can't count the times I would believe his stories. One day he came into the house, looking so distressed and said, 'guess what?' When I looked equally distraught; enough to please him, he paused and said somberly 'they shot Lincoln!' He could trap me in the same episode over and over again. How could I be so gullible? Nevertheless, I loved his many tricks."

A pastor's wife often finds herself caught in a balancing act of family time over against a congregation's needs. Even though surrounded by people, loneliness can erupt into an unsettling need. Like other women a pastor's wife knows the need for close friendships, a trusted friend with whom to share feelings and frustrations. Mildred contends, "I survived and God has been so good to us. In many places our social contacts were beautifully met in a pastor's fellowship and in Bible study groups."

During one pastorate when only two of their boys remained at home, Mildred did the unexpected. She learned about a hostess position available in a large tearoom. It required mid-day hours and only for the duration of the 'Christmas rush.' So, she became the hostess (which fit like a 'glove,') and described it as "an enjoyable experience that I got paid for doing."

However, occasionally the sheep in the congregation deem it appropriate to make inquiries about the shepherd's family, which precludes follow-up advice.

Such was the situation on a Sunday morning. "I hear you are working," the `sheep' said to Mildred. "Is that right?" Mildred nodded in assent as the sharp knife of guilt twisted within. Another probing question followed, "Do you really have to work?" Mildred wanted to defend her actions explaining that their two married sons and families were coming for Christmas and she wanted to help out. Her hearts desire was also to purchase a gift for Aymond using her own money. Demonstrating the Lord's kindness, she merely answered "No, I don't suppose."

The 'sheep' felt duty bound to get Mildred in line, and retorted, "Well if you are working and don't need to, you are taking a job away from someone who really needs the money!" Mildred smiled graciously, but later commented on such experiences as leaving you either 'bitter or better.' "Hopefully it helped me understand others."

Priceless family times gratefully outstrip life's minor annoyances. When living in Chicago, a long remembered 'happy happening' took place when Aymond returned from a series of evangelistic meetings. Mildred and the boys went to O'Hare airport to welcome him home. The boys wanted their Dad to receive a celebrity greeting upon arrival. Each one, including Dawn, made individual posters, 11 x 14 inches and fastened them to long sticks. Dennis, a little embarrassed by the whole thing, produced one that measured 3 x 4 inches fastened to a 12-inch stick and said simply, "*Welcome home, Dad.*"

Several of the airport employees joined in the fun and made their own signs: 'going my way, Armand; no hope for the pope, we vote for Armand; thumbs down on LBJ and Ho! Ho! You're our Joe.' The family signs, which Aymond has lovingly kept in his possession, read: 'Hi Aymond, glad you're home; Rah rah! Pa Pa! Welcome home Dad—why you stay so long, we protest; and Y-e-a-h! Good to have you home again.' On one of the signs, probably drawn by his artist son is displayed a picture of Aymond's famous thumb. An interested spectator asked one of the boys, "how long has he been gone?" The answer: "a week!" A much-loved celebrity Dad returned to his family.

One of Mildred's tender remembrances of life with Aymond was when traveling in the car with him. Poetry flowed from his exceptional memory as they drove along the highway. Anything from "Abou Ben ADHem; That Dog; Pass it On; Robert Moffat's "My Album Is A Savage Breast," and "Building for Eternity."

Her thoughts return to their much-loved Addison Street Church in Chicago and an additional example of Aymond's incredible memory. "At the front of the church sanctuary, a large semi-circle of thirty individuals stood as Aymond welcomed them into the church membership. He went down the line, shaking each person's hand, calling them by name and never once referring to his list." She feels his memory is a beautiful thing, yet "as a pastor's wife, my inner concern was, what if he doesn't remember?" Other pastor's wives can empathize, knowing she breathed a sigh of relief as he finished, while marveling at his ability.

Mildred shares a few perceptions based on years of observing her humble pastor husband. In her words: "Ay took his call into the ministry very seriously—it was the most important thing in his life and he gave it his very best. He didn't think it beneath his calling to do things others had not remembered, such as turning on and off the lights, shoveling snow and cleaning the sanctuary after a service of forgotten bulletins and candy wrappers. If light bulbs needed replacing, and the clock required a new setting, he took care of it.

"In other areas he never felt he was the 'ruler of *his* church.' He respected the ideas and capabilities of the boards with whom he worked. He often commented on church administration saying, 'why should I push an agenda in opposition to men who excelled in their careers. Men like the treasurer of the International Harvester Company, the owner of a steel factory, teachers, professors, and other pastors in the congregation. All proved to be dedicated to the work of the Lord and sincere in their serving.' In turn they often asked for and respected his input. He enjoyed a good relationship with his church staffs— not always seeing eye to eye, but realizing their work as the Lord's, and enjoyed a harmonious relationship."

When Aymond became executive director of the Midwest Baptist Conference, he frequently traveled, speaking at various churches in his district. As a result, Mildred and the two younger boys divided their time between the Cumberland Church in Mount Prospect and the Northbrook Church where she shared her gift of music with the congregations.

Asked if she faced an adjustment when she no longer filled the role of 'the pastor's wife,' her response spoke highly of her ministry attitude. "I didn't feel any less of a person. I was with friends as well as other women whose husbands were away on military duty." During this era of ministry, Mildred and Aymond purchased their first home in Skokie, IL., including a fireplace. She enjoyed working part-time in the Midwest office, as well as serving on call as an organist at several funeral homes. "During this period, I had a freedom that was pleasant, but felt delighted when I had the responsibilities of a pastor's wife again."

When they considered returning to Door County she had a few misgivings, but realized this as God's plan. "All our churches treated us well and Bethel Church in Ellison Bay was not an exception." During this pastorate Mildred began a Newcomers Bible Study that ultimately reached 75 women, mostly new to the area. This group met together for nearly twenty-eight years, thanks to Mildred's insight. In this setting, women found a place to feel at home, make new friends and study God's Word.

Her approach to ministry sums up a servant attitude. "We realized we would not amass a fortune in ministry, yet God supplied our needs if not all of our wants! During these years, Aymond's highest salary was $12,000.00 annually when he served as Executive Secretary of the Midwest district. We never cease to wonder how God blessed us even as we struggled financially. At times God supplied through the giving of dear friends who quietly helped. The churches we have served have showered so much love and care upon us that we feel most unworthy.

"Would I choose to be a pastor's wife and marry Aymond all over again? Without a doubt."

Aymond poignantly reflects on the formidable task of balancing responsibilities between church and family. "Church came first and the family had to fit in. Today the pendulum is pointed in a different direction. I don't know if I could do it differently, but I'd like to spend more time with my family."

He continues, "When a woman marries a pastor, she needs to enter this role with her eyes open, as the ministry is team work." (Mildred may have had her eyes open, yet never imagined she would one day spend a week's vacation on Cape Cod, helping Aymond organize his file system. Notwithstanding she felt, 'at least we were together.')

"Overall," he confirms, "my kids turned out well. In retrospect, I would have prayed more for them, and attempted to 'sneak' in some fun things, not detracting from the ministry. My main concern is, do they see the love of God in me?"

Frequently the 'older' generation is asked how their life would be different if they could live it over and the usual reply is 'I would live it exactly the same.' Aymond prefers the opposite answer. "I can't understand such a reply. I know there would be many changes in my life. I would have appreciated my mother more (that's for sure); my personal life would be more disciplined; financial matters would be wiser and I would be a better father to my children, and husband to my wife."

Mildred includes the following note on 'things he loves:'

- Purple martins and the farm out-house.
- Being home and hearing "I love you."
- A soft sweater and a hug.
- Dick's hand-me-down clothes and Howard Weborg's hats.
- New thoughts during the night and preaching.
- Florida in the winter (only) and flea markets.
- Young people and TV sports
- Dennis' jackets, shoes and oatmeal cookies.
- His grandchildren and wonderful daughters-in-law.
- Vibra harp music and Phil Austin's art.
- Dan's photography and having friends meet his boys.
- Snakes and snoring gophers.
- Playing Crazy Eight and a good joke.
- Buttermilk and rice pudding.
- Showing off his boy's places and security.
- Old tools, collectibles and his barn.
- His study and his truck
- Grubby clothes and his garden.
- Mysterious happenings and lightning.
- Door County picnics and Saturday morning in Florida.
- Turkey necks, lemon pie and maple nut ice cream.
- Working hard and vacations at the cottage.
- Sisters, family, and church friends near and far.
- Hitting golf balls and going to bed early.
- Teaching Sunday School and sitting in the last row at church.
- George Rice and Delmar Dahl
- Telephoning hurting people.

- Mildred. (Although she didn't include this, Aymond would place her name at the top of this list).

Chapter 14

Favorite Stories of Aymond's

he adult Sunday School at Bethel Baptist Church is about to begin. The coffee and goodies accompanied by chatter and laughter come to an end as Mark Weborg spontaneously ignites them into joyful singing. As everyone takes their chair, they see the teacher of the day, seated on his stool. Waiting impatiently to begin teaching the lesson, is Aymond. He glances at his watch and then at Mark and breathes a sigh of relief when Mark tells him 'its' his.

Without wasting a minute, Aymond begins speaking with firmness and clarity getting immediately to the point. Both hands raised and fingers spread wide he emphatically shares his concern about the moral condition in our world, his concern for young people, and the need for adults to show love to them. He continues to teach for 40 minutes when he leans back, folds his arms, clears his throat and proclaims, "Know something? I'm done!"

A close friend, Dale Seaquist, introduced Aymond in the morning service one Sunday prior to his preaching. He concluded by looking at Aymond and saying, "You've got so many stories. Why don't you write them down?"

As a result, the following are a few morsels from his 90 + years of stories. Using his fantastic memory he loves to relate stories, yet unfortunately, it's impossible to capture his expressions, empathetic gesturing, impish grins and at times compassionately sad demeanor. It is hoped the reader can picture Aymond telling these stories with his great compassion and humor.

One of his stories concerns a tragedy he witnessed; yet at the same time it illustrates his compassion for others.

"One day while I was in my study at the Wilmington church, sirens screamed as a city fire truck raced to the park two blocks away. I sensed something serious must have happened so I left my office and ran to the site. There I saw the body of a nine-year-old boy who had been found lying at the bottom of the park pool. Medical personnel worked frantically to revive him. As they worked, I asked if they minded if I prayed, and they readily agreed."

The following day the Wilmington Morning News carried the story of the tragic event, including the fact that nearby a preacher prayed. Aymond continued, "Eventually, the doctor present, sadly rendered his verdict. The boy's life could not be saved. It was a somber group of onlookers as they listened to the doctor's words. I couldn't help but think, the boy is still all there— every muscle and organ, but that mysterious thing called life is gone, and he is no more. This became the basis of a sermon I preached soon after this tragedy, "I Have A Life to Live.""

Live it he has, along with his matchless sense of humor that endears him to many. A leader of mischievous fun, he retains many stories proving this capability. While a student at Bethel College, he joined the male chorus, traveling with the group presenting concerts in many churches across the United States.

On one trip, the bus driver stopped at a small crossroads store and gas station. Aymond and friend Clifford Dickau headed for the 'necessary' facility located outside the store. As they entered the 'john,' Aymond noticed a window open and his mischievous nature surfaced. "I wickedly suggested we leave the door locked and jump out the window; just to see what might happen.

"Great idea! We jumped out and casually sauntered over to join the group who hadn't missed us. When the other guys decided it was time to visit the john before returning to the bus, the door was surprisingly locked. They pounded on it and shouted 'open up!' Finally, someone walked to the rear of the building and saw the open window, crawled through it and unlocked the door."

As the bus rolled down the highway, finally on its way, the men could not nap or even sing a few tunes until the burning question of the moment became answered, which without a doubt was, 'who among us could be the culprit who locked the john door?' The perturbed singers, bent on knowing the answer, would not relent until the guilty could be detected. After many miles, involving Sherlock Holmes methods, it was avowed the criminals sitting innocently in their midst were none other than Aymond and Clifford. A hastily formed bus trial determined their punishment and the jury ordered their pants removed and kept off until the stop for the evening!

The culprits with pants in place and antics aside, traveled on another male chorus tour where a more meaningful experience occurred. The men presented a concert in a Bridgeport, Connecticut church and spent the night in various homes. Aymond mentioned to his host that he'd be interested in seeing Fanny Crosby's grave site. He remembered the song leader in his home church giving a brief background on the author prior to singing a song she had written . . As he introduced one of her hymns, the leader said, 'Even though blind, she wrote as many as 1000 hymns.' Intrigued, Aymond read bits of her life history and learned she was buried in Bridgeport, Connecticut.

"It's a good thing my host took me to the cemetery or I'd never have found it," Aymond relates. "When we came to the area, my host said, 'this is it.' I didn't see grave stones of any size until he pointed to the ground. There lay a small marker, about 30 inches long, 12 inches wide and 6 inches high. Compared to the area surrounding, it appeared insignificant. The inscription simply read and printed on 3 lines, `Aunt Fanny—year of birth and death—She has done what she could.'

"As I stood looking around, a large, tall, imposing monument stood nearby; the resting-place of P.T. Barnum, the circus magnate. A short distance from his grave, was another figure of a man (shorter than P. T.) standing on top of a monument. It was a life size figure of Tom Thumb, P. T. Barnum's most famous character."

Aymond summed up the experience. "We know that P. T. Barnum brought happiness and a joyful experience to many of his day. But as I stood there, I could not help but reflect upon Fanny Crosby's ministry of song which brought such spiritual blessing reaching unto the eternal."

Preparation for ministry began as a teenager for Aymond and continued when on assignments at Moody and Bethel College. He felt the male chorus trips and Moody preaching experiences on street corners; jails and churches were 'gr-r-e-a-at experiences.'

One day several groups of Moody students returned from their ministry assignments and gathered together to share their experiences. The leader of one group related an unplanned ending to his illustration as he spoke at a mission. According to Aymond, "The guy had been speaking on Romans 6:23: 'The gift of God is eternal life.' He illustrated it by taking out his pocketknife and saying, 'what is a gift? You don't pay for it, just take it.' He continued saying, 'I will give this knife to any one who will come up and just take it.' No one came, so he repeated the offer three times. Finally, one man half-drunk, seemed to understand, went forward, and took the knife. The problem was that another student, Joe was supposed to come up and take it, but the dumb cluck didn't, and he lost his knife. This struck me funny!"

When a pastor in Wilmington, Delaware, Aymond preached at the Skid Row Mission. By now a seasoned mission speaker, yet he could not predict the unpredictable. At the end of his message he asked the audience, "How many of you know you are saved; that you have accepted Jesus as your Savior?" A few hands raised upwards. A man standing next to the aisle did not raise his hand, but extended it across the aisle and with a loud voice said, 'I'm only half-saved.' Aymond failed to understand this kind of logic, but the man left the mission and he never saw him again.

Illustrations gone haywire, unpredictable skid row ministries and disruptive bugs infiltrating a church meeting, all contribute to a speaker's dilemma. Aymond tells how they were overruled one evening. "It was June and bug season in Homestead, Wisconsin where I held special meetings. The congregation kept ducking their heads and I thought, `oh, oh, there goes the service.'" In spite of bugs, Aymond preached his heart out, ending with an invitation for those who desired to accept Christ, to come and stand in front of the church. "I did something I've never done before or after. I walked down to a troubled man, whom I had met that day put my arm around him and asked if he would like to make a decision. His brother was standing next to him and said, 'I think tonight is the time for you.' At this, the man responded to the invitation. As a result, twenty-five people came forward to accept Christ, followed by a baptismal service for fifteen." A confirmation of the irrelevance of bugs when weighed against the power of the Holy Spirit!

Weddings can also give rise to the unexpected. Aymond tells of an unusual experience when he performed a marriage in the bride's home. "I had counseled the couple previously. The groom arrived at the last minute due to heavy traffic in Chicago. I quickly reviewed some basics, and reminded him to say 'I do' in three places of the ceremony. When the time came, I asked the groom, do you take _____ as your wedded wife, etc. He answered, 'I do, I do, I do,' and again, 'I do, I do, I do.' I'm sure the people thought this was part of the ceremony; no one even smiled. I never mentioned this to the groom, or anyone else until many years had passed."

An unanticipated facet of one known to possess the ability to deliver a thirty-minute sermon is brevity. Aymond's friend Delmar became accustomed to his occasional abbreviated speech. Speaking to Aymond on the phone, Delmar knew it would be a short conversation consisting of "Yah, yah, ok," unless Aymond wanted to talk. "Then I knew I'd better listen!" maintains Delmar.

This was exemplified prior to the wedding ceremony of Delmar and Barbara Dahl. Aymond would soon unite them in marriage at the Sister Bay Church. The evening was unbearably hot. As the male chorus dressed in stifling hot tuxedos provided beautiful music prior to the service, Aymond stood with Delmar in a small hall outside of the sanctuary. He gave Delmar some prudent and concise advice. "Don't be in a hurry. At best it will be very short." At that, the wedding took place and Aymond kept his word.

Aymond's stories came not only from pastoring, but also from his helpful husband role. While living in Chicago, he stopped at the grocery store on his way home to purchase items of food for dinner. Standing in the check out line waiting his turn, he observed a woman who literally shoved a man aside to get ahead of him. "I expected him to explode in anger, but not so.

He turned to me and smiled saying, "If a woman had not done the same to me a few years ago, I would not be here today; I would have been killed."

Aymond recounts the man's reason. "He was standing on a curb waiting for the streetcar to come. When it arrived, the people rushed forward making certain they had their place in the car. Just as he stepped on the first step, a woman pushed him aside. She was the last one that could possibly get in. As the car went on its way, he stood looking after it, fuming within. A short time later, a gasoline truck lost control; crashing into the streetcar filled with people. Electric sparks ignited the gasoline, enveloping the car. When the doors could be opened, the passengers stood in place packed together tightly—all dead. No wonder the man did not mind being shoved around."

The following tales of calamities endured by Aymond, leaves one to wonder how he survived into his nineties.

He tells that at three or four years old he had his first accident. "A pile of trees lay in the woods. The opposite end of the tree root was thin and you could stand on it, you see, and 'yip, yip, yip!' I stood on one and 'root toot!' It bounced, causing me to fly up, and I fell and broke my arm," he illustrated graphically.

The Anderson's didn't have a phone, and he isn't sure how his mother notified the doctor. However, he recalls seeing two headlights on the doctor's car (the first car Aymond had seen) as it pulled into their yard. The doctor came into the kitchen/emergency room, wasted no time, and gave a painful pull on Aymond's injured arm in an attempt to set the bone correctly. He then told Mrs. Anderson to bring her son into his office for an X-Ray.

While he sat immersed in the comfort of his mother's arms, Aymond recalls the x-ray room being small and pitch dark. "I think his x-ray machine was called Roentgen rays. As he turned the crank and looked into the machine he could see my arm. This caused bright sparks to fly everywhere," In spite of the 'fireworks' and the inability to produce pictures, the doctor seemed satisfied he had pulled the bone correctly into place and applied a cast to Aymond's arm.

While working on a farm as a teenager Aymond experienced a 'bolt out of the blue.' It was a sunny July day and the *bright* blue sky displayed only one cloud. As Aymond busily shocked grain, a brilliant flash, without warning transpired, followed by one terrifying loud clap of thunder. The lightening bolt shattered a telephone pole a short distance away. "Even though I stayed on my feet, a team of horses dropped to the ground." Aymond was left astounded that he and the horses survived this close call.

An additional story from Aymond's adult life bears proof he has kept the medical community active. While living in Ellison Bay, he visited a neighbor to borrow an item. Aymond recounts the near disastrous incident that began in the attic and concluded elsewhere. "I was ready to climb back down the steps, having taken a different route than when I came up. A large piece of Styrofoam lay on the floor near the stairs. I took one step on it and quickly learned there wasn't a floor under it! The Styrofoam exploded with a loud bang and down I went, not able to do anything to stop my fall. I made a somersault in the air, landing on the coffee table, bounced off that, and ended up on a couch. Probably the fall took only a few seconds. One leg seemed to hurt a lot, but fortunately x-rays showed no breaks."

From accidents to additional stories from Pastor Aymond:
The flu epidemic of 1918 resulted in an unusual story told to Aymond by the Nelson family who attended the church in

Marinette, Wisconsin. Stationed in France, Mr. Nelson served with the armed forces. While there, he was caught in the midst of the appalling flu epidemic. The flu struck his camp with such severity that it became impossible to care for all the patients, nor could the facilities accommodate everyone. When a patient became terminal, they moved him to another area, leaving him to die with no further medical attention.

Mr. Nelson soon became seriously ill with the flu. When his condition became terminal, the officials transferred him to the 'end of the road' area to die. As he lay unconscious, a medic bringing in another patient noticed the wedding band on Mr. Nelson's finger. Realizing he must be married and probably a father, he ordered him taken back to the hospital facility for treatment and the possibility of recovery. A few years later in Marinette, WI, Aymond met L.L. Nelson an attorney, husband of the church member. Aymond observed he still wore his wedding band. "He was the man that had been left to die. Grea-a-a-t story!"

The Wilmington, Delaware church held a series of meetings with a visiting pastor. At the conclusion of his preaching he gave an invitation for salvation while the congregation sang a hymn. As Aymond stood on the platform, he noticed a tall, elderly man with gray hair in the audience. "I had never seen him in church or the neighborhood. Suddenly he slammed the hymnal shut, said a few words and stalked out. After the service, the person who had stood beside him related, "when the congregation sang, he uttered 'I can't sing that;' seemed upset and left.'"

"This bothered me, wondering if I would see him again, therefore I prayed I would be given that opportunity. The very next day, he walked by our house and I hurried to catch up to him. We spoke about the service of the previous evening and I talked with him about receiving Christ. He replied, "if I could believe as you do, I would get down on my knees right here on this sidewalk.'"

"We spoke briefly and he continued on his way returning the next evening for the service. At the beginning of the invitation he said loudly, 'Jesus, I come.' He came forward and I went with him into a side room where we could meet privately. We had not talked long, when I realized he had a rather unusual spiritual experience. I went back on the platform and told the people this man had something helpful to tell them.

"He shared with the congregation about walking out when they sang 'Jesus I come,' and also told of meeting me the next day. After speaking with me, he related that he continued on home, and as he walked he took the New Testament he carried with him out of his pocket. It opened to John 5:40 where he read 'You will not come to me that you may have life.' He said to himself, 'is that the reason I am not saved, that I don't come?' Then standing on the sidewalk, he cried out loud, 'Jesus I come.' Instantly he said, the heavy burden left, and he felt as though he had wings. Soon, he was baptized and thereafter had an uplifting testimony.'"

A story with a somber ending stands in contrast to the previous. During her high school years Aymond's sister lived in the home of the school principal, Professor Bell and his family. They became good friends, and continued to keep in contact at Christmas after the family eventually moved out of town. Aymond visited his sister one Christmas season and she gave him her friends Christmas letter to read.

One paragraph captured his attention. It read, "Near retirement as I look back upon my life, I regret I did not plan with more perspective in mind. I just went from day to day, with no high goal in mind." "This man was not a failure in his profession," Aymond commented. "It is so sad to come to the end of life and feel one has missed the essentials. I have used this when I have spoken to young people and it was the basis of a gre-a-t sermon, I Have A Life to Live."

Two of Aymonds favorite stories on Christian love follow:

Eva Booth of the Salvation Army planned to minister at a precinct jail one Sunday morning. It was used mainly for the inebriated as an overnight facility before taken to the 'big house.' Aymond claims "these places are just awful, smelling of vomit, urine, etc." Eva arrived before visiting hours. As she waited, a commotion took place around the corner and as they came into sight, she witnessed two police officers roughly dragging a struggling, screaming, and cursing woman.

Viewing the scene coming towards her she frantically wondered what to do. She didn't have time to pray for wisdom, but in describing the incident later said, "it was an angel that pushed me toward the woman as she passed by, and I planted a kiss on her cheek. At once the woman wrenched herself free, lifted her hands upward and cried out—'who kissed me?' At that she began to sob, lifted her dirty apron to her face, wiped her eyes and went meekly with the officers."

Eva decided to visit her the next day. She asked the matron for the woman who had been brought in the day before. The matron replied, "Yes, she is here, but we wonder about her; she keeps asking everyone 'do you know who kissed me? No one has kissed me since my mother died.'" Eva replied, "It was I!"

The matron brought the woman in to Eva. She now had on a clean gown, her hair was combed, and her eyes appeared bright. Seeing Eva she said, "Do you know who kissed me yesterday?" Eva answered, "It was I." With relief the woman related her story.

Her mother had died in the basement of a run down home as she lay on some rags under a stairway. Before she died she drew her little daughter to her, kissed her, and said, "Who shall take care of you when I am gone?"

The woman told Eva, "No one has kissed me since that time, until yesterday." Eva then told her about Jesus who loved her. The woman willingly accepted Him as her Savior and became a radiant Christian, ministering to other women who experienced a similar life.

The second story took place in an orphanage.

A little girl did not fit in at the orphanage, but according to rules, the supervisor and head nurse could not remove her without a legitimate reason. One day the two nurses walked on the grounds and watched as the child climbed a tree whose branches hung over the wall extending to the outside grounds. They saw her reach as far as possible on a branch as she placed something white at the very end, then scrambled down.

The nurses said to each other with a note of satisfaction, "Now we can have her transferred to another facility, because she has broken the rule of no contact with outside parties." They hurried to the branch, reached up and removed a small piece of paper. The supervisor read it and without a word handed it to the other nurse. When she finished reading she stood silent, for the little girl had written these words: "To anyone, who finds this, I love you." Without a word the two walked away. "There is no argument or ill feeling when real love is shown," Aymond validated.

When a student at Moody, Aymond listened intently as a man named Shabaz spoke to the students and told of an experience which demonstrated his strong faith in Christ. His message made a deep impression on Aymond and later it became the basis for a sermon he preached, "The Name of Jesus Christ."

Originally from Persia (Iran), Shabaz came to America for his education. Here, he heard the good news of Jesus Christ and was converted to Christianity. Subsequently he returned to Persia and served as a missionary to the Moslems. This could have proved dangerous, as Christians were often killed because of their faith in Christ. However, Shabaz officially had gained the respect of the Moslem leadership presumably because he was one of 'their' own, well educated and a brilliant speaker.

Shabaz told of a risky experience when he attended an annual meeting of about 3000 Moslem leaders of Persia. Invited to speak following the business session, he began by saying, "I have listened to you telling of the devotion you have to your prophet Mohammed. Now I wish to talk regarding my prophet, Jesus Christ. I know in your faith you consider Abraham, Moses, David, Jesus Christ, and the great prophet Mohammed. Tell me what you consider the basic virtue is in a prophet. The leaders responded with answers such as, he should not lie, kill, etc. At that point, beginning with Abraham, then Moses, then David, he drew a line through the names written on a large blackboard, proving from the Karon they did not qualify. He bypassed the name of Jesus Christ and spoke of Mohammed, proving from the Koran he did not qualify. He then drew a line through his name.

He concluded his speech by saying, "I have spoken relative to your great prophet. Now I want you to speak regarding the One I consider the true prophet. Does He qualify? What faults do you find in Him? Shabaz stood quietly and waited, and waited. Minutes went by. No one spoke. Then he quietly declared, "His name alone remains clear." The meeting ended and the large assembly left silently refusing to consider the thought provoking questions, preferring they hang without answers concealing their unbelief.

On a lighter note, the focus is off Pastor Aymond and onto Uncle Aymond as his niece Jo Anne Kollofski confirms her uncles mischievous nature. (Written in a 1977 writing course).

POSTS AND POCKETS

To have an uncle who is 6' 4" tall, who has a booming voice that you obey before you decide whether or not he is teasing, and who is also 'studying to be a preacher' is at age eight, somewhat unnerving.

At that time, we lived on a small farm in central Wisconsin. Every summer our uncle came to visit. One of Aymond's favorite jobs was mending fences and replacing rotten posts.

One day, Aymond, my brother, Edward, and I set off to a corner of the farm where the fence needed mending. Our father had been there previously to leave a new post leaning against each weathered one. Aymond carried various tools; a hammer, a pliers and a wirecutter. In his pockets were nails, screws, and whatever else he deemed necessary for the job.

When we arrived at the site, Aymond set his equipment on the ground at the base of the nearest post. Although Edward and I stayed near Aymond as we played, we were hardly conscious of his progress down the line of posts.

Then, "JoAnne, would you please get my hammer? I left it about four posts back. It's on the ground at the bottom of the post."

I turned, ran to the post, stooped to reach for the hammer, and froze. It was positioned on the coiled body of a huge, green, sleeping pine snake. I stood shaking, hands covering my face, imagining, in my child's mind, what it would have felt like to actually have touched the massive reptile.

"Aymond!" I accused loudly when my voice returned, "You set that hammer right on top of a snake! You did it on purpose, didn't you?"

Aymond strolled slowly back to where I stood. He reached casually into his shirt pocket. "How about a piece of candy?" he asked. He took out a round, white, fluffy morsel and with great deliberateness, popped it into his mouth.

Of course, we knew this trick, too. He was really throwing the 'candy' over his shoulder. At each new post hole he had been collecting fat, white grubworms to 'share' should he be able to create just this situation.

Chapter 15

This and That

*A*ymond has collected a myriad of quotes and articles, which he keeps in his efficient file system. The following are some of his favorites, which he refers to as 'this and that.' In many, the author is unknown.

"Truth forever on the scaffold, wrong forever on the throne,
Yet the scaffold sways the future, for God who standeth in the shadows
Is keeping watch over His own."

"Some want to live within the sound of church or mission bell
I want to run a rescue shop, one yard this side of hell."
C.E. Studd

"God carefully reviews all of our tomorrow's
Before He allows them to come to us."

"The angels from their realms on high, look down with wondering eye,
That where we are but passing guests, we build such strong and sturdy nests
But where we hope to stay for aye, we scarce take time one stone to lay."

"If I have wounded any soul today, if I have caused one foot to go astray,
If I have walked in my own willful way, dear Lord—forgive.
Forgive the sins, I have confessed to thee, forgive the wrong I did not see,
Guide me, help me, and my helper be, dear Lord—Amen."
Sung by McQueen on WCCO radio, Minneapolis, MN every A.M.

"I cannot, God never said I could,
God can and always said He could."

"Isn't it strange that princes and kings and clowns that caper in sawdust rings
And common folk like you and me, are builders for eternity?
To each is given a box of tools, some lumps of clay and a set of rules
And each must fashion ere life is flown, a stumbling block or a stepping stone."

"God has already put under His feet
That which threatens to come over our heads."

"How precious is the Book divine, by inspiration given,
Bright as a lamp its pages shine, to guide our souls to heaven,
This book through all the tedious night of life, shall guide our way,
Till we behold the clearer light, of the eternal day."

"Thirty Five" (one of Aymond's favorites)
"The sun was hot
The sky was bright
And all July was overhead
I heard the locust burst in flight,
Six weeks till frost, it said."

"Klondike" Robert Service
"I wanted gold and I sought it, I scrabbled and mucked it like a stone
Was it famine or scurvy, I fought it, and I hurled my youth into the grave.
I wanted gold and I got it, came out with a fortune last fall
Yet somehow life is not what I thought it, and some how the gold is not all.
Carve your name above the shifting sands, where the steadfast rocks defy decay
But all you can hold in your cold dead hands, is what you have given away.
Build your pyramids skyward to stand, gazed at by millions, cultured they say
But all you can hold in your cold dead hand, is what you have given away.
Count your wide conquests on sea and land, heap up your god; hoard as you may,
But all you can hold in your cold dead hands is what you have given away."

"When God wants something done He creates a child,
Then waits."
"I took a piece of plastic clay, and idly molded it one day
And as my fingers shaped it still, it moved and yielded
to my will
I came again when days were past, behold the clay was
hard at last
It still the early impress bore, and I could change it never
more.
I took a piece of human clay, and idly molded it one day
With all my cunning skill and art, young chills soft and
tender heart
I came again when days were gone, behold it was a man
I looked upon
He still the early impress bore, and I could change him
nevermore."

"There is no one who can fully, fully, fully understand
himself, and I make the statement, the longest journey
we can ever take is not to Hawaii, but the journey within.
We don't want to take it, because we see things there
that are not good." Aymond Anderson

Quotes Aymond used in his sermon series on Christian love.

1. The mills of God grind slowly, but they grind exceedingly fine.
2. Whom the god's would destroy, they first make them mad.
3. When it gets dark enough the stars will come out.
4. The bee fertilizes the flower it robs. There is always compensation.
5. A kind word will warm three winter months.
6. A harsh word will freeze the flowers in July.

Chapter 16

The Value of a Human Being

A favorite sermon of Aymond's
Preached in the First Baptist Church
Sister Bay, Wisconsin
(unabridged)

The format of learning at the Moody Bible Institute was two-fold. The student was taught in the classroom and then was assigned to go out in society and minister.

In my second year I was assigned to minister at the Cook County jail. It was a large facility—hundreds of prisoners.

At that time there were three men—each of them had killed a man. Their trials were short, and each was sentenced to die in the electric chair. One of these, Joseph Frances had received Jesus Christ as his Savior. He was highly respected by his fellow prisoners in the cellblock where they were confined. One Sunday morning, I came to that cellblock. One of the prisoners came up to the bars and said to me, "There is going to be a meeting of the State Board of Pardons and Parole in Springfield to again consider the fate of these three men." Then he said, "Will you go down to that meeting and speak in behalf of Joseph Francis?"

(To continue the story of Joseph Frances, please refer to chapter 1.)

Continuing:

"These reflections and feelings lingered with me for a long time and resulted in the basis of one of my first sermons. The title of which was "The Value of a Human Being."

INTRO: In Psalm 8: 3 and 4 we read "When I consider thy heavens, the work of thy fingers, the moon and the stars, which thou hast ordained; what is man that thou art mindful of him?"

In the light of such company, man must have great value. We will list a few.

I Personal Value

1. Man is a distinct, unique, one of a kind personality. Proof of this, are his fingerprints and his DNA description (possession).
2. There are problems that make it hard to grasp this great value of a person.

Here are two.

    a. Immensity. The vastness of the universe staggers the mind. Millions of not only stars, but of galaxies. How can one person even be compared?
    b. Multitudes (of people). There are five billion people on this planet. If we had space to place that many dots on some surface, how would you be able to find a specific one?

3. So man needs help to give assurance, that in spite of the above, the one has value. The source of assurance is the Bible. Consider Galations 2:20. "He loved me and gave Himself for me." This sets me apart from all others. Further more, all scripture is personal. (Every promise in the book is mine). As one said, "The Bible finds me!"

4. Again Galations 2:20. The love of God 'is as broad as humanity, and as narrow as myself.' Isaiah 45:22. As someone said, "The sun shines upon a single bunch of grapes to ripen it as though it had nothing else to do."
5. So now, we can apply the law of economics. According to the scarcity or abundance of a commodity, so is the value. For example, we don't pick up pebbles on a gravel walk and put them into our pockets, but if there is but a penny lying there, we pick that up. (There are not as many pennies as pebbles). A baseball card featuring Honnus Wagner was expected to bring $45,000.00, but at an auction of rare items, it brought $420,000.00.

So we conclude that each person has great value, as there is but one exactly like him. When that young man went to the electric chair, its something went out of this world that would never appear again.

II. An Unknown Value

Louis Pasteur said, "When I see a little child, it inspires me with two feelings, a feeling of deep tenderness, because of what this child is and a feeling of the highest respect because of what this child may become. In every child there is always the unknown factor."

In a home in Little Falls, MN, a baby boy was born. The mother sat and rocked that baby she held in her arms, and maybe had thought that he might grow up and follow in his fathers footsteps; But in her wildest dreams she never could think that one day, he would fly across the Atlantic all alone and become the most famous man in all the world—Charles Lindberg. Another mother—same scenario—rocking chair. Never dreams that one-day he would walk on the moon—Neil Armstrong.

III The Known Value

1. The baby is grown and lives his life—his value unknown. For our day—dramatic and most likely never will be repeated.

2. Two individuals—Princess Diana and Mother Theresa. Untold millions testified of their worth and contribution to their lives.
    On a lesser note, we heard people say, "If it had not been for that person, I would not be what I am today. They made a great contribution in my life. In this group are parents, teachers, and friends.

IV The Long Range Value

1. This vital value makes the picture complete.
    In Mark 8:36 are these words, "What shall it profit a man if he gains the whole world and loses his soul." A lesson to learn. It is not so important how many toys we collect, bank accounts, boats, cars, stocks and bonds, etc. But the greatest lesson is so live that we end with our future in heaven with all of its glory that is endless.

2. The words lose his soul!
    This speaks of mans greatest value. Mark 8:36. Standing on a high vantage point in Montclair, New Jersey, one can see the skyline of New York City. If one could say, I own these tall buildings, I own those great ships coming into the harbor. Yes, I own it all, yet my soul is lost. All is loss. In Matt. 12: 11, Jesus was criticized because He healed on the Sabbath day. He said, "If such a one of you shall fall into a ditch on the Sabbath, you will pull it out. Isn't a man worth more than a ship?" We go to the skid row area and see the derelicts—seemingly so worth-

less. Yet, if placed on God's balance scale of value, that worthless one outweighs the world!

3. Body and soul
   The body is thinking of man in the earthly sense—the soul—in the basic and eternal sense. The body is the earthly vehicle in which the soul abides. The body is called a tent and a tabernacle; a building. II Peter 1:13, 14. II Cor. 5:1, 4. The soul lives just as well without the body. Ecc. 12:7. The body returns to the dust and the spirit, to God who gave it.

4. Again what is the soul?
   Not some mystical part of you. It is the real you. Mark 8:36 "What shall I profit. . . if we gain the whole world, but he himself is lost." The soul (the real you) lives in a body. You are distinct from the body. The body will die—totally and return to dust, but you will live on. You give direction to the body. Rom. 12. You are in charge of it. You are responsible for the actions of the body. A dead body does nothing. Why? Because the director is gone. The body only does what its master dictates.
   It is the soul (the real you) that whispers of its immaturity. Ecc.3:11. "The Lord has put eternity in the heart." Why, the pyramids—the mummies—to preserve the bodies for the soul.
   I visited an Indian graveyard in Minnesota. At the head of every grave was a small shelter in which food could be place to be used by the one in the grave.

5. It is the soul (the real you) that communicates with God. I have a small book, the title of which is "The Third Strike." It is the story of a man who became addicted to drink. In his despair he jumped into the Hudson River to die. He was rescued and taken to Bellevue Hospital. The staff tried to help him, but he did not seem to respond to their efforts. The staff met with him and ex-

pressed their concern in his apparent lack of coopera-
tion. He replied "My sickness is the sickness of my soul,
and the soul is God's exclusive domain."
What is the basic difference between man and animal?
Man alone worships and prays. Modern man ignores the
value of man. They say four legs are better that two.
Destroy an eagle egg and you pay a fine of $5000.00.
Destroy endless numbers of the unborn; so what? These
have no value. But judgment will always follow.

V. Ultimate proof of man's value.

1. Seen in Redemption. What is the story of the Bible? It is
    the story of God's redemption.

2. Why? Because of man's great value in god's sight.

3. It is God's great concern that man be restored. God had
    that in mind from the very beginning. Man was created
    in God's image. Nothing could be greater!

4. If any one doubts his value in God's sight, he should
    take a long close look at Calvary.

5. The crucifixion. Listen carefully to what Jesus says. There
    are seven, but I mention three. "My God why have you
    forsaken me?" The cry of desolation, necessary to ac-
    complish man's salvation. Again, "It is finished!" Now
    all has been done and accomplished in complete salva-
    tion. Again the words of the thief and Jesus' response.
    "Please remember me, Jesus." "I surely will. Today, you
    are going to be with me in Paradise. Not just you are
    going to be in Paradise, but with me!" The result we can
    see Jesus and the thief walking arm in arm into Para-
    dise. What a glorious thought for all!

6. Then look at nature's response. Great darkness—terri-
    fying. 'The sun refused to shine.' When God the mighty
    creator died for man, this creature's sin. The stars come
    out to view the awful sight and the blades of grass caught
    the drops of blood shed that man might be redeemed.
    How great must be man's value in God's sight. How tragic
    that any should be lost as His God—has done so much.
    "It is a fearsome thing to fall into the hands of the living
    God." Hebrews 10:31.

Conclusion

What should be the attitude, the concern of every Christian? I believe that it should be that shown by Robert Moffat,
missionary to Africa.

He was home on furlough and speaking in a church in Eng-
land. After the service a young girl came up to him with an
autograph album and asked him to write something in it.

This is what he wrote:

> My album is a savage breast
> Where tempest rage and shadows rest
> Without a ray of light
> To plant the name of Jesus there
> And see the savage kneel in prayer
> And point to a world more bright and fair
> That is my soul's delight.

Addendum

The following are but a few reflections taken from the past and the present in place of the possible abundance of expressions from Aymond's many friends. Comments from the Addison Baptist Church's 100th anniversary celebration:

> **Henry Wingblade**, former president of Bethel College, St. Paul, MN: he recalled when Aymond did a parody on himself as president. "People laughed 'til tears rolled down their faces."
>
> **C. Emmanuel Carlson**, executive director Baptist Joint Committee on Public Affairs: "Aymond confided a keen sense of inferiority and it was a battle whenever he went into the pulpit although the response of the community to his preaching was immediate. Aymond has a clipped and dramatic delivery and communicates a vivacious personality. His style distinctly is his own making; effectively capitalizing on his rich gifts and experiences—even to the effective use of his flat thumb."

John R. Seaquist, Sister Bay, WI: "Beside being a man of God and a strong speaker, Aymond is possessed of a remarkable insight into the everyday cares of people. The practical result of this insight, is the down to earth quality of his messages and their applications to real life situations. When listening to him a person feels a desire to move from where you are, to what you ought to be."

Other friends:

Jeff Weborg, Bethel Baptist Church, Ellison Bay, WI: He observed when Mildred and Aymond came to Ellison Bay, they came ready to serve. "As a new Sunday School teacher, I received willing and ready help from Aymond. I'd call him on the phone with a question. His reply would be `Yah, yah, yah, come on over.' I of course went and he took me up to his office and asked `what can I do for you?' I would explain, and his answer to me was to pull a book off the shelf, hand it to me and say, "read it."

Pastor Delmar Dahl: "Aymond excitedly preached what He believed. He secretly helped many people. He believed in me even though we have a 20 years + age difference. He was a good mentor. When I asked him for advice, his response would be 'Yup, tell me—go ahead.' He kept my confidences. Daily he had an excitement about Christ. He just plain loves Jesus. Aymond and Mildred became one in the best sense of the word."

Al Johnson from Sister Bay's renowned restaurant placed an invitation in the area newspaper announcing a birthday celebration for Aymond. Many friends came to Al's restaurant (where the goats munch on the rooftop grass), and celebrated inside with rolls and coffee.

The respect shown for Aymond came not only from Al Johnson, but also from his son **Lars Johnson.** Lars approached Aymond saying, "we will probably have another child and if it's a boy, would you mind if we used your name?" Surprised,

Aymond agreed to it. Before long an announcement appeared in the newspaper announcing the birth of Thor Aymond Herman born to Lars and Jill Johnson.

According to **Mildred**, Aymond has not always enjoyed his name. "When very young and people, especially teachers asked his name, he replied, Aymond, to which they questioned, `What?' Finally, his name received some respect in the life of a tiny baby."

Aymond's associate in the ministry at Addison Church in Chicago was **George Rice**. George writes: "God has used several men to encourage, guide and help me in my lifetime. Aymond Anderson is one of those men. As a fledgling youth pastor in a city ministry, I was given the opportunity to work alongside this man. He was my teacher—he was my mentor. Aymond taught me, yea showed me by his life, what unconditional love meant. He loves the sinner and the saint, the lovely and the unlovely, the up and outer and down and outer, the clean, the not so clean, the poor and the rich. All in the same manner!

"He showed me what a consistent prayer life should be. Even today when I meet him, he inquires about young people who were part of our ministry over thirty years ago and tells me he continues to pray for them.

"He has always been supportive and encouraging. He continues to be my cheerleader today.

"When I think of Aymond, Philippians 4: 8 and 9 come to mind:

"Finally, brothers whatever is true, whatever is noble, whatever is right, whatever is pure, whatever is lovely, whatever is admirable, if anything is excellent or praiseworthy—think about such things. Whatever you have learned or received or hear from me, or seen in me—put it into practice, and the God of peace will be with you."

"Aymond has led the kind of life that would allow him to say `put into practice what you've observed in my life.' He has been a real example of a Christian man to me—but most of all, he is my friend!"

Aymond's compassion for those hurting has been felt deeply by many. One afternoon while waiting for him to make a phone call, I overheard him ask Betty Weborg for some 'blessing fish.' Following the phone call, he explained that he would leave shortly to visit a friend going through a painful experience and would take some fish to them contributed by the Weborgs.

The lonely, the grieving, those in crisis; the Lord has touched them through Aymond's compassion. The hurting in the surrounding community have felt his caring, but also friends a long distance from him geographically, receive many telephone encouragement calls. Often times these friends have been laid low by critical attitudes, ignored by others, or simply forgotten in the whirl of a 'busy' and sometimes uncaring life style.

The tender heart of Aymond often has caused tears to flow as he observes the anguish of others. He said, "I can truthfully say I have compassion for others, even though I know so little about their hardship, sorrow and loneliness and am grateful for this emotion."

It has been my God given privilege to sit at the dining room table at "Friendly Acres" and record his recollections of the past, and bring it to the present. His facial and verbal expressions plus his great delight in relating many stories have been captivating. Occasionally he would look at me and say firmly, "Now put that pen down and just listen!" I obeyed.

The gift of Aymond's keen mind coupled with his sense of humor and rooted in his love for Jesus Christ, has been demonstrated to me in his unswerving and disciplined life of prayer. I thank God for this opportunity. Donna B.

His name is Aymond and he walks with God!

To order additional copies of

From Pitchfork
to Pulpit

Please visit our web site at
www.pleasantword.com

Also available at:
www.amazon.com
and
www.barnesandnoble.com

Printed in the United States
26112LVS00001B/397-423

9 781414 102504